RELIGION IN LIFE CURRICULUM
Edited by Edward A. Fitzpatrick, Ph.D.

FOURTH GRADE TEACHERS PLAN BOOK
AND MANUAL

BOOK OF THE HOLY CHILD (Grade One)

LIFE OF MY SAVIOR (Grade Two)

LIFE OF THE SOUL (Grade Three)

BEFORE CHRIST CAME (Grade Four)

THE VINE AND THE BRANCHES (Grade Five)

THE MISSAL (Grade Six)

HIGHWAY TO GOD (Grades Seven and Eight)

Accompanying this Series is the RELIGION IN LIFE CURRICULUM for grades one to six and PRACTICAL PROBLEMS IN RELIGION for grades seven and eight.

Fourth Grade Teachers Plan Book and Manual

A School Sister of Notre Dame

Member of the Faculty at the Diocesan Teachers College, St. Paul, Minnesota

Designed for use with the
HIGHWAY TO HEAVEN SERIES
of Catechism Textbooks

ST. AUGUSTINE ACADEMY PRESS
HOMER GLEN, ILLINOIS

Nihil obstat:
    R. G. BANDAS,
        Censor Deputatus

Imprimatur:
    ✝ JOANNES GREGORIUS MURRAY,
        Archiepiscopus Sancti Pauli

April 7, 1933

This book was originally published in 1935 by The Bruce Publishing Company.

This edition reprinted in 2018 by St. Augustine Academy Press.

ISBN: 978-1-64051-032-6

EDITOR'S FOREWORD

This book tells the story of the Hebrew people and of God's relation to them as narrated in the Holy Bible. It is principally the story of the Promise of a Redeemer which God made to Adam in the Garden of Eden after the Fall, and of the fulfillment of that Promise in the birth of Christ, our Lord. It is what we know familiarly as Bible History. Its point of view is indicated in the title of the textbook which is used with this manual, *Before Christ Came.* The history of the Hebrews is most significant as a preparation for the Messiah, Christ.

The central thought in this manual is the coming of this Redeemer, the Messiah, who would save Israel and all men. It is to this idea that the teacher should continually return. In her preparation for each lesson, and in the conduct of each lesson, the question which the teacher should always keep in mind is: What relation has this lesson to the Messianic prophecy and the Messianic tradition? That will give unity to the work of this grade and lay a strong foundation for the succeeding grades.

The history of the Hebrew people was a training school in which God was the teacher in a special sense to His chosen people. The lessons of that history are available to us, and teachers would miss an opportunity if they did not take advantage of these lessons. But the teacher must always keep in mind the historical example that has furnished the basis. She must keep referring to this example, Job, or Noe, or Melchisedech, whoever it may be. That is what will make clear that it is Bible History that we are teaching.

The incidents in the Old Testament, as the source of Bible History, suggest a study of some distinctly Christian doctrines.

Consequently, in addition to the ethical application and practical conduct of life, there are studies of the sacraments, for example, Baptism. The teacher will keep clearly in mind that the study of Christian doctrine is suggested by the Biblical incident, and that this incident is not the basis of doctrine. In the cases listed that basis is clearly Christ Himself, and no confusion must be permitted even inadvertently to creep in on this point.

The author of this manual, Sr. Mary Agnesine, has shown great pedagogic shrewdness in enriching the Biblical incidents while at the same time keeping them central. We are all grateful to the St. Paul Diocesan Teachers College for the opportunity it has given to help the author to discuss the problems of this manual and to secure the benefit of helpful criticism of a very practical nature.

EDWARD A. FITZPATRICK

Marquette University Catechetical Institute
June 5, 1935

TO THE REVEREND INSTRUCTOR

The Highway to Heaven Series, of which this book is a part, does not aim to eliminate or minimize the teaching of religion by the priest. It does, however, offer a new and more interesting approach to the same truths that have always been taught by means of the Catechism or Bible History alone.

The Reverend Instructor who goes to the classroom once or twice a week, might, if he wishes, follow one of two courses outlined below. In either case the teacher and pupils co-operate with him, so that the best possible results may be obtained from each lesson.

1. The instructor may let the class read and work out the entire lesson prescribed for the week, under the direction of the teacher. He then uses the instruction period to survey the week's work, to assure himself by questions, that the pupils understand the lesson and all it implies, and then proceeds to explain at length one or more of the outstanding truths which are suggested by the story or by the questions at the 'end of each lesson.

2. He may give his instruction first, on the lesson itself or any particular part of it, and then let the children under the direction of the teacher develop the subject more fully by means of the little exercises and activities suggested in the text. In that case he reviews their work at the beginning of the next instruction period and asks questions such as those suggested at the end of the lesson to assure himself that they have grasped the meaning according to their ability.

How to Proceed

Take, for example, Lessons 3, 4, and 5, on the Creation (second week) according to the first plan. The teacher has read the three stories with the children and worked out as many of the assimilative activities as she has found time to include. The instructor, on his arrival, asks a few important questions about the stories themselves and perhaps also about the meaning of the sand-table project and drawings they may have made. He asks the questions following the lesson and adds others of his own. Then he proceeds to dwell on the creation of man according to the image and likeness of God, speaks of the soul and its importance, and perhaps of the terrible consequences of the sin of Adam and Eve for the whole human race.

Now let us take Lesson 6, Cain and Abel, according to the second method. The instructor first reviews the most important points of his last instruction, possibly looks at some of the classwork in connection with the last lesson, and then introduces the new subject. He may choose to talk about the story of Cain and Abel itself, and draw therefrom the more important lessons. He may wish also to dwell on the evil of entertaining wicked thoughts, such as jealousy, revenge, etc., using as specific example the story of Cain and Abel (which the children will read from their own books with all the more interest afterwards). The teacher spends the rest of the week developing and reviewing more at length the story itself, the important and underlying moral and doctrinal truths brought out by the instructor, and their application in the student's own life.

However, where the Reverend Instructor is in close daily touch with the work of the class, he may choose the discussion of the life problems or some other phase of the lesson for his own share of the work. He is thereby afforded opportunity to apply his teachings more intimately to the individuals and, incidentally, to know his class better. In any case, it is he who chooses from the lesson the most important truths to be taught, leaving the work of review and further development to the classroom teacher.

CONTENTS

EDITOR'S NOTE TO THE REPRINTED EDITION:

In reassembling this *Religion in Life Curriculum*, we thought it best to include excerpts from the curriculum overview volume, titled *Curriculum in Religion*, which was published in 1931 as the basis for development of the fleshed-out Teachers Plan Book and Manual before you. In that original volume, the entire curriculum for first through eighth grades were laid out in basic outline form, with attention given to the main focus, goals and resources for each grade. You may find that some of the resources listed in these excerpts did not find their way into the current manual. However, we felt it would be helpful to the teacher (or parent) to see a summary of the intended vision for the current year.

In the appendix found at the rear of this volume, we have also provided a comprehensive listing of all the recommended resources found in this manual, to which we have added notations showing the most frequently used and/or most helpful resources, as well as those which can be found online.

Lastly, please note that most of the recommended student readings (that is, those which would have been found in the various school readers listed throughout the student text) have been assembled and printed under one cover in the new *Magnificat Readers* which accompany this series. In addition, we have done our best to find and scan the pages of *The Catholic School Journal* and *The Journal of Religious Instruction* recommended herein; find these on our website at www.staapress.com/hth-teacher-resources.

Lisa Bergman

St. Augustine Academy Press
March 2018

The following section is an excerpt from the book "A Curriculum in Religion,"
included for the convenience of teachers as a way of familiarizing themselves with
the basic goals laid out for the Religion in Life Curriculum for the Fourth Grade.

RELIGION IN GRADE IV

Main Interest: Old Testament History

THE content of the fourth grade centers around Bible history. In order to bring it within the experience of the child, it will be told in a series of biographies. In order to provide for connection and continuity, either the text or the teacher will provide the account of the situation in which the principal figure was concerned. In this way an adequate historical background will be furnished for each character and historical continuity provided.

The characters and topics selected for study are:

Outline of Main Topics

I. *Creation of the World*
   1. The creation
   2. Adam and Eve
   3. Cain and Abel
   4. Noah

II. *The Founders*
   1. Abraham
   2. Melchisedech
   3. Isaac
   4. Jacob
   5. Joseph
   6. Job

The purpose of this study is not a complete history of the Jews, but a review of the principal characters in Jewish religious history, with emphasis on biography. The main points to be secured are three: (1) the conception of a Messiah in Jewish history, with the Messianic prophecies; (2) the situation among the Jews at the time of Christ, and (3) the basis for their rejection of Christ. It will be a real challenge to the ingenuity and skill of both textbook and teacher to do this.

Quotations

In this grade the quotations to be memorized relate especially to the Messianic prophecies; some others of significance as a preparation for the Mass. Some quotations are given to illustrate the wisdom literature of the Jews. A few psalms are added for their significance in themselves as well as to illustrate the work of David the singer; others may be substituted:

"But Melchisedech the king of Salem, bringing forth bread and wine, for he was the priest of the most high God. Blessed him, and said: Blessed be Abram by the most high God, Who created heaven and earth" (Gen. xiv, 18–19).

"Who is there among you, that will shut the doors, and will kindle the fire on My altar gratis? I have no pleasure in you, saith the Lord of hosts: and I will not receive a gift of your hand. For from the rising of the sun even to the going down, My Name is great among the Gentiles, and in every place there is sacrifice, and there is offered to My Name a clean oblation: for My Name is great among the Gentiles, saith the Lord of hosts" (Mal. i, 10–11).

Psalm lxxxix.

Psalm lii.

"The voice of one crying in the desert: Prepare ye the way of the Lord, make straight in the wilderness the paths of our God" (Isa. xl, 3).

"For a CHILD IS BORN to us, and a Son is given to us, and the government is upon His shoulder: and His Name shall be called, Wonderful, Counsellor, God the Mighty, the Father of the world to come, the Prince of Peace" (Isa. ix, 6).

"Therefore the Lord Himself shall give you a sign. Behold a virgin shall conceive, and bear a Son, and His Name shall be called Emmanuel" (Isa. vii, 14).

"Behold My Servant, I will uphold Him: My elect, My soul delighteth in Him: I have given My spirit upon Him. He shall bring forth judgment to the Gentiles" (Isa. xlii, 1).

"They parted My garments amongst them; and upon My vesture they cast lots" (Ps. xxi, 19).

"And I said to them: If it be good in your eyes, bring hither my wages: and if not, be quiet. And they weighed for my wages thirty pieces of silver" (Zach. xi, 12).

"They shall not leave anything thereof until morning, nor break a bone thereof, they shall observe all the ceremonies of the phase" (Num. ix, 12).

"AND THOU, BETHLEHEM Ephrata, art a little one among the thousands of Juda: out of thee shall He come forth unto Me that is to be the ruler in Israel: and His going forth *is* from the beginning, from the days of eternity" (Mic. v, 2).

"Judge me, O God, and distinguish my cause from the nation that is not holy: deliver me from the unjust and deceitful man.

For Thou art God my strength: why hast Thou cast me off? and why do I go sorrowful whilst the enemy afflicteth me?

Send forth Thy light and Thy truth: they have conducted me, and have brought me unto Thy holy hill, and into Thy tabernacles.

And I will go into the altar of God: to God Who giveth joy to my youth.

To Thee, O God my God, I will give praise upon the harp: why art thou sad, O my soul? and why dost thou disquiet me?

Hope in God, for I will still give praise to Him: the salvation of my countenance, and my God" (Ps. xlii, 1–6).

"I will wash my hands among the innocent; and will compass Thy altar, O Lord:

That I may hear the voice of Thy praise: and tell of all Thy wondrous works.

I have loved, O Lord, the beauty of Thy house; and the place where Thy glory dwelleth.

Take not away my soul, O God, with the wicked: nor my life with bloody men:

In whose hands are iniquities: their right hand is filled with gifts" (Ps. xxv, 6–10).

"And one of the Seraphims flew to me, and in his hand was a live coal, which he had taken with the tongs off the altar.

And he touched my mouth, and said: Behold this hath touched thy lips, and thy iniquities shall be taken away, and thy sin shall be cleansed" (Isa. vi, 6–7).

"Blessed art Thou, O Lord the God of our fathers: and worthy to be praised, and glorified, and exalted above all for ever: and blessed is the holy name of Thy glory: and worthy to be praised, and exalted above all in all ages" (Dan. iii, 52).

"The fear of the Lord is the beginning of wisdom. Fools despise wisdom and instruction" (Prov. i, 7).

"My son, hear the instruction of thy father, and forsake not the law of thy mother" (Prov. i, 8).

"My son, forget not My law, and let thy heart keep My commandments" (Prov. iii, 1).

"For whom the Lord loveth, He chastiseth: and as a father in the son He pleaseth Himself" (Prov. iii, 12).

"Go to the ant, O sluggard, and consider her ways, and learn wisdom" (Prov. vi, 6).

"Six things there are, which the Lord hateth, and the seventh His soul detesteth:

Haughty eyes, a lying tongue, hands that shed innocent blood.

A heart that deviseth wicked plots, feet that are swift to run into mischief.

A deceitful witness that uttereth lies, and him that soweth discord among brethren" (Prov. vi, 16–19).

"My son, keep my words, and lay up my precepts with thee. Son, keep the commandments, and thou shalt live: and my law as the apple of thy eye:

Bind it upon thy fingers, write it upon the tables of thy heart" (Prov. vii, 1–3).

Activities

The stories of the Old Testament offer excellent opportunities for spontaneous dramatization in the classroom, and for a more formal literary dramatization. Suggestions are contained in Sr. Aurelia and Fr. Kirsch's *Practical Aids for Catholic Teachers*, pp. 234–238. Suggestive dramatizations are offered (pp. 238–242) of

Cain and Abel
The Building of the Ark
Noah's Offering — the Rainbow
The Story of Joseph
The Story of Moses*

The student might select a special character in Old Testament history to make a booklet about him or her, presenting orally to the class toward the end of the semester or year a summary of what he learned. Sand-table projects, posters, calendars, booklets, plays, stories, collection of poems, pictures, even movies furnish fresh methods of approach, or methods of reënforcing more conventional methods of learning.

Pictures

For the picture study of this grade, reënforcing the main topic of the grade, there are two excellent sources of material. First are the 120 Old Testament pictures by J. James Tissot, published by the American Tissot Society, and another are the pictures by Gustave Doré illustrating the Paradise lost. For textbook pictures we have already referred you to the pictures in the *Katholische Schulbibel* by Fügel. In this grade students should become acquainted with Sargeant's *Prophets.*

---

*The steps in analyzing a story either in preparation for a dramatization or for writing a biography are illustrated in the article, by Miss Margaret Canty, "Joseph the Dreamer" in the March, 1931, issue of the CATHOLIC SCHOOL JOURNAL.

Religious Vocabulary

Special care must be taken to see that the child's religious vocabulary is increased in connection particularly with the main topic of the grade, and that the new words are taught as the need develops and in the actual situation. Care should be taken to review words previously learned and to be sure a correct meaning is given to them on the child's own level. The words should grow in connotation as his religious knowledge and experience increase.

Words that will generally be taught in this grade are:

Messiah (Messias)	psalm	prophet
prophecy	Genesis	disobedience
sacrifice	Babel	famine
Pharaoh	plagues	Sinai
tables of stone	idolatry	manna
ingratitude	bondage	deliverance
priest	anointed	sanctuary
Ark of the Covenant	captivity	Babylon (ion)
miracles	sacred scriptures	Pharisees
Paradise	Palestine	Israel
Juda		

Each teacher will be required to make up her specific lists for her specific children. No stress need be placed on the spelling of these words. They may be left on the board for reference.

Poems

The poems suggested for the fourth grade carrying along the fundamental idea of the curriculum and furnishing reënforcement for the central interest of this grade are:

Father in Heaven, We Thank Thee
The Word True, Sister Agnes Finley
This Above All to Thine Own Self be True, Shakespeare
Our Heavenly Father, Rev. Frederick W. Faber
Absolom, Nathaniel Parker Willis
Psalm 150, David
The Meadow of Prayer, Edward F. Garesché, S.J.
That Holy Thing, George MacDonald
Worship Old and New, S. M. Pierre
By the Waters of Babylon, Christina Rossetti
Heroes, Denis A. McCarthy
St. Peter, Eileen Duggan
A Sorrowful Sigh of a Prisoner, C. Rossetti
Mary Magdalene, Christina Rossetti
The Catechism of the Clock, Eleanor C. Donnelly
Why the Robin's Breast was Red, James Ryder Randall
Wishes for My Son, Thomas MacDonagh
The Helper, Rev. Hugh Francis Blunt
My Wish, Rev. Francis J. Butler
Each Daily Task, Very Rev. T. L. Crowley, O.P.
A Christmas Carol, Adelaide A. Procter
All of It, Rev. Hugh Francis Blunt
The Mother's Quest, Rev. Hugh Francis Blunt
The Burial of Moses, Cecil Frances Alexander
Adam and Eve, Progressive Series, Third Reader
Evening Prayer, William Allingham
As Little Children, William V. Doyle, S.J.
Mistletoe, Rev. John B. Tabb
A Child's Thought of God, Elizabeth Barrett Browning
The Children and the Angels, Mary E. Mannix
Content and Rich, Rev. Robert Southwell, S.J.
The Vision of Baltassar, Lord Byron
Guardian Angel, Cardinal Newman
Christmas, Nahum Tate
Ballad of Trees and the Master, Sidney Lanier
Blessed Candle, Joseph Kinney Collins

He was the Word that Spake It, John Donne
The Caliph's Magnanimity
A Legend
A Child's Evening Prayer, Samuel Taylor Coleridge
How Children Should Live, Isaac Watts
The Queen of May
Sheep and Lambs, Katharine Tynan
Speak Little Voice, Rev. Michael Earls, S.J.
Holy Communion, Speer Strahan

Additional poems should be used emphasizing the public life of Christ which is the center of interest in the grade. Children should be encouraged to "learn by heart" as many poems as possible. All should be required to learn some; many of the poems should be left to the student's own taste. The more difficult poems will be read to the class by the teachers; some poems will be read for their general idea without detailed study, and some poems will be studied in detail. Poems dealing with the same subject in earlier grades should be recalled to mind after the first reading of new poems. The poems suggested above, with others, are included in *Religious Poems for Children, Intermediate Grades,* (Bruce).

Aspirations and Brief Prayers

As opportunity offers, the following aspirations and brief prayers or others will be taught. One might be selected and written on the board each month, calling attention to it as opportunity permits. The Psalms furnish an almost inexhaustible source for additional suggestions. The students might prepare aspirations of their own. The following are selected from the Old Testament:

1. Have mercy on me and hear my prayer (Ps. iv).

2. O Lord, my God, in Thee have I put my trust: save me from all them that persecute me and deliver me (Ps. vii).

3. I will give praise to Thee, O Lord, with my whole heart (Ps. ix).

4. Preserve me, O Lord, for I have put my trust in Thee (Ps. xv).

5. My God *is* my helper, and in Him will I put my trust (Ps. xvii).

6. To Thee, O Lord, have I lifted up my soul. In Thee, O my God, I put my trust, let me not be ashamed (Ps. xxiv).

7. I will bless the Lord at all times. His praise shall be always in my mouth (Ps. xxxiii).

8. Forsake me not, O Lord my God: do not Thou depart from me. Attend unto my help, O Lord, the God of my salvation (Ps. xxxvii).

9. Have mercy on me, O God, according to Thy great mercy (Ps. l).

10. Blessed art Thou, O Lord the God of our fathers; and worthy to be praised, and glorified, and exalted above all for ever: and blessed is the holy name of Thy glory: and worthy to be praised, and exalted above all in all ages (Dan. iii. 52).

11. And now, O Lord, think of me, and take not revenge of my sins, neither remember my offences nor those of my parents (Tob. iii. 3).

Prayers

As the child develops, the form of prayers he will learn will change. The form of morning prayer will undoubtedly change from the simplest form to the use of the liturgical prayers of the Church. This will be generally the development. There will be, of course, an increase in the number of prayers, so that by the end of the elementary school the student will be acquainted with the principal prayers of the Church.

1. Morning Prayers
2. Evening Prayers
3. Grace before meals
4. Grace after meals
5. Act of Contrition
6. Act of Faith
7. Act of Hope
8. Act of Charity
9. Stations of the Cross
10. The Gloria
11. Prayers of thanksgiving and praise from the Psalms

Hymns

Hymns are an important factor in reënforcing the general religious instruction and training, valuable for their own content, and, if properly taught, add an element of joy in religious instruction that is quite important. The child should, at the end of instruction, know the great hymns of the Church. For the fourth grade there is suggested the following to be sung within the voice range of the children:

1. Canticle of the Three Children (Dan. iii. 26)
2. Benedicite (Dan. iii. 57)
3. O Come, O Come, Emmanuel
4. Drop Down, Dew

5. God the Father, Who Didst Make Me
6. Souls of Men Why Will Ye Scatter
7. How Blind Thou Art
8. Jerusalem The Golden
9. Now Doth the Sun Ascend the Sky
10. Sing Praise to God
11. God, the Only Good

Liturgy

The main interest of this grade will be the history of the Jews in the Old Testament, and will furnish valuable concrete information regarding the sacrifice in the religious sense. It would therefore seem to be desirable to emphasize in this grade the Christian altar and its ornaments, and incidentally other parts of the Church, the credence table, the Communion rail, the pulpit, the baptistery, and the sacristy.

Useful supplementary material for the study of various aspects of the liturgy will be found in Father Dunney's *The Mass*, (Macmillan Co.), and Father M. S. MacMahon's *Liturgical Catechism*, (Gill & Son, Dublin), and *St. Andrew's Missal*.

Religious Information

There are certain facts about religious persons, vestments, ceremonies, and institutions that are a part of the equipment of every cultivated person, as well as essential or at least supplementary to religious practice. These need to be taught, and specific provision should be made for the instruction.

One is surprised often to find adults who do not know what INRI means, or *Alpha* and *Omega*, or even IHS, why the Mass is said in Latin, or who some prominent character in the Old or New Testament is. The teacher should use every opportunity to give such information whenever she discovers there is need for it.

In this grade will be taught, in addition to what the teacher discovers to be the need of the pupil, the following:

Facts about the Old Testament

I. The Books of the Old Testament
  1. The Historical Books (Genesis to Esther)
  2. Poetical Books (Job to Ecclesiasticus)
    a) Poetical
    b) Didactic
  3. The Prophetical Books (Isaias to Malachias)
    a) Major
    b) Minor
  4. Supplementary, Historical (1–2 Machabees)
II. Divine Inspiration of the Bible
III. Books in the Catholic Bible omitted in Protestant Version
IV. Priesthood and Sacrifice in Old Testament
V. Hebrew measures and money
  1. Shekels, drachmas, bin, etc.

An indispensable guide to the teacher is Pope's *The Catholic Student's Aids to the Studies of the Bible*, Vol. I (Rev. Ed.), which includes an English translation of Pope Leo XIII's Encyclical on the Study of the Bible, *Providentissimus Deus*, and also Vol. II.

A specially useful source of questions and answers for this part of the course on religious information is Father John F. Sullivan's *Externals of the Catholic*

Church, Her Government, Ceremonies, Festivals, Sacramentals and Devotions (Kenedy), and Father Conway's *The Question Box.* The new *Catholic Dictionary* is especially useful. For reference the *Catholic Encyclopedia* is indispensable. This heading is placed in the curriculum so that the teacher will realize the relative importance of this informational background to the main purpose, and will not give it undue emphasis at the expense of weightier matters. Information should be given as information.

Religious Practice

A definite part of the program in every grade is to build up the practice of religion in every grade and have the development cumulative throughout the grades. Wherever teachers see opportunity to build up Catholic practice, they should do so. Teachers must not confound the lessons that may be essential and the actual practice in the life of the child. The pupil should understand the importance of interior disposition.

In the assignment to grade the purpose is to provide a specific time to see that the practice is established and understood. In some cases the habit will have been established. The cumulative listing of these practices is to emphasize the fact that they are not taught or established once and you are through with them. The practice must continue to be stimulated until it is "securely rooted in the life of the individual." There should be emphasized in this grade:

1. Morning Prayer
2. Evening Prayer

3. Regular attendance at Mass on Sundays
4. Attendance at Mass on all holydays of obligation
5. Angelus
6. Bowing at the name of Jesus
7. Tipping hat or bowing as one passes church
8. Tipping hat when one meets Priest or Sister or other religious
9. Monthly Communion or more frequently
10. Keeping spirit of Lent by sacrifice
11. Saying Stations of the Cross

Practical Life

The translation of the religious knowledge, practice, and attitudes in the day-to-day life of the child must always be an objective in religious education. The elevation of the actual daily life of the individual to a supernatural plane will come about through the character of the individual's motivation. This must be a matter of development; the child must be taken, however, where he is. The lines of development are indicated but the more specific content is left for the experimentation of the first year. A teacher should always take advantage of any actual situation, and should always strive to meet difficulties which her children as a group are confronted with, no matter whether it is included in the course of study or not.

1. Do a good turn every day for the love of God.
    a) Daily examination of conscience at night.
    b) Daily specific review of day's thoughts, words, or deeds.
    c) Weekly complete examination of conscience

for confession or as a preparation for spiritual Communion.

d) Daily expiation for the temporal punishment due to sin.

2. Cultivation of virtuous life.

3. Cultivation of school virtues.

4. Promotion of corporal and spiritual works of mercy.

Special attention is directed to the chapters on "The Christian Rule of Life" and "The Christian Daily Exercise" of the *Catechism of Christian Doctrine* approved by the Cardinal, Archbishops, and Bishops of England and Wales, and directed to be used in all their dioceses.

Christian Doctrine

In this grade Christ is studied as He is anticipated in the Old Testament. God's relation with the Hebrew people generally is the content. The Ten Commandments are reviewed here in their historical setting. The visits of angels to earth are met concretely here as a basis for later study of angels, and in review of first-grade material. The Messianic prophecies and in general the expectation of Israel are emphasized. The prayers of the Old Testament are noted in the Psalms particularly, and particularly in such portions of them as are found in the Mass.

Texts and Teaching Material

An adequate basal text on the Old Testament in the fourth-grade level is not now available. The syllabus contains the detailed outline of the instruction.

It is expected that the experience of the first year will give an adequate basis for a text especially prepared for the course written with a biographical emphasis.

The following newer texts may prove useful:

Bible Stories for Children, Sister Anna Louise.

Bible History of the Old and New Testament with Compendium of Church History, Sister Anna Louise.

Compendium of Bible and Church History, Brother Eugene.

Illustrated Bible History, Rev. Ignatius Schuster.

A Child's Garden of Religion Stories, Rev. P. Henry Matimore.

Wonder Stories of God's People, Rev. P. Henry Matimore.

Old Testament Rhymes, Rev. Robert Hugh Benson, (Longmans Green & Co.).

The Bible Story, Rev. George Johnson, Rev. Jerome D. Hannan, and Sr. M. Dominica, O.S.U. (to be followed by *Bible History* and *Church History*).

Valuable suggestions may be secured from stories in school readers. A partial list indicating range and technique of material is given at the end of this grade.

RELIGION IN GRADE IV

INTRODUCTION

To You, Who Are Teaching *Before Christ Came*

Use your plan book regularly. This plan book is intended for your specific use. It may contain many suggestions with which you are already familiar. In that case it will give you a great deal of satisfaction to have this confirmation of your own experience in teaching religion. On the other hand, you will very likely find much that will help you make your religion classes more interesting and vital. The suggestions given for each lesson are the outgrowth of long personal experience and intimate contact with other teachers of religion. They are not intended to hinder you in exercising your ingenuity but rather to help you organize your work with the least possible loss of time and to assist you in bringing new and interesting material to the classroom each week.

You are urged, therefore, to read this manual carefully and frequently, and to make the best possible use of your opportunity to improve upon your methods of teaching and to combine your own ideas with those presented here, so that there may be nothing left undone to make the study of religion the most delightful and most effective of all the subjects taught in the school.

Keep in Mind the End

The end to be achieved according to the method here proposed, is not project work, nor booklets, nor plays, nor other interesting activities. All these are but *means* to an end. The end is to teach or present religious truth so interestingly, so convincingly, so full of spirit and life, that it will take hold of the mind and heart and will manifest itself eventually in every phase of the child's life.

1

The Textbook

Before Christ Came has for its main interest the Old Testament, viewed in the light of the Great Promise made to Adam and Eve in Paradise. The stories are told as nearly as possible in the simple, dignified language of the Holy Bible. Doctrinal truths, already learned to a large extent in the first three grades, are reviewed or newly presented as an outgrowth of the story rather than as isolated facts. A careful study of the book will bring to light the following outstanding features:

1. The Old Testament is studied not merely as a group of stories but in the light of the Great Promise made by God in Paradise, a foreshadowing of the greatest event in the history of mankind, the coming of the Redeemer.

2. The doctrine is developed naturally from the story (Christ's own method) and in consequence the religious truths — usually presented in question and answer form in a cold, isolated manner — are better understood and more easily applied to life situations.

3. Religious instruction reaches out into every phase of child-life and correlates naturally with every other activity in and out of school. For, "Religion is life."

4. There is a distinct and consistent aim at character training viewed as an outgrowth of the teachings of Christ and His Church rather than as a separate function without doctrinal foundation.

5. The latest and best pedagogical methods, which take into consideration the age, ability, and interests of the child, are used, making the study of religion more pleasant, vital, and effective than is possible by the old methods.

The Units

The book is divided into Units or natural divisions that can be easily grasped by the child. The Introductions to the Unit usually take a backward look to view what has already been learned and to indicate the connection between past lessons and those to follow. They are the strong links that bind together the various parts into a well-organized, consistent whole. The teacher should strive to keep this purpose in mind and help the children to focus attention from time to time on the picture of the Old Testament as a whole.

The Aim of the Week's Lesson

It is important for the teacher to have clearly in mind, as she presents each lesson, the specific aims of the week's work. For that purpose the aim is stated in this manual at the beginning of each lesson. With that in mind, the teacher and pupils will know exactly the purpose of the various activities which might otherwise easily deteriorate into work without definite purpose.

Preparation

The success of each lesson depends largely upon the teacher's preparation. It is, therefore, of the greatest importance that she look over her work for the week, note any suggestions she may desire to carry out, and proceed to gather and prepare the required material. Not every suggested activity need or should be carried out to the letter. If she knows of better or more interesting ways of developing the lesson, she should, by all means, use them.

The activities of the week, if planned ahead of time, will easily fit themselves into the work of different periods of the day or to a bit of outside study. Frequently the children may be encouraged to carry out directions and find information on their own initiative.

Approach to the Lesson

The teacher should plan to approach the day's lesson in religion from various angles so as to make the pupils look forward eagerly to further developments. Instead of beginning every morning with, "Now take your books and we shall continue our religion lesson," she may say nothing whatever about the book for the time being, but read a little poem, let us say, that really strikes the keynote of the thought to be developed that day. The poem is discussed and finally the teacher says: "Now let us see what our book has to say about the subject." Stories, hymns, and particularly pictures may be used in the same way. For example, the picture of *Ruth, the Gleaner,* or Millet's *The Gleaners* may serve to open the discussion for Lesson 43. At another time, review questions might lead up to the day's lesson. The aim is, of course, to arouse interest and attention. The important thing, therefore, is not so much to have a different approach each day as to plan carefully the most interesting and helpful way of beginning the religion lesson. The approach must always move toward the specific lesson of the day.

The Story

Ordinarily it will be found most convenient to begin the week's work with the Bible story itself; but it may also serve as a development of the lesson or as a summary at the end of the week (see suggestions for Lesson 2). Frequently the story will have to be read several times. Sometimes it should be read just for an appreciation of the simplicity and dignity of the Biblical language (Lesson 2). In fact, it is advisable to summarize practically every lesson with a final reading of the story.

The story need not always be read during the religion period Another period may well be used at times; for example, the reading period. Sometimes, too, it may be read at home.

The stories should be made as real as possible. Talk about them, help the children over their difficulties, explain new words, ancient customs, etc. And keep in mind always the unifying thought — the promise of the Redeemer, and God's loving care for the nation out of which the Redeemer was finally to come.

The Questions on the Story

The questions following the story are intended to ascertain whether the pupils have grasped the lesson. They may be used also to stimulate thought, by proposing them ahead of time and having the pupils read quietly to find the answer. Again, the teacher may use the questions to convince herself that the story has been read by the pupils at home or during another period, and that it has been thoroughly understood. They may be used orally, assigned as written work, or omitted altogether if there is no further need for them. The omission should not be frequent, however.

Topics for Discussion

Such topics as "Ask Yourself," "Are You a Missionary," etc., and the quotations and other selections, offer splendid material for character training. The aim of the teacher must be not only to get the right answer, but — and this is more important — to direct the children to think for themselves, to recognize their own needs and shortcomings, and, above all, to acquire the right viewpoint, so that their attitudes may be directed accordingly and they may desire also to *do* what is right.

This process of training must be very simple and may be very slow. The teacher must lead on carefully and tactfully, always being careful that the pupils modify their conduct not only because they please her thereby but gradually and principally because, being children of God, they wish to do right for His sake. An occasional little practice cheerfully and well done will do more good than too many practices and resolutions that may easily become burdensome and distasteful. Individual help will be of great benefit where the class is not too large. Some of the pupils will also get help and direction from their parents, if they are encouraged to take their problems home for further consultation.

Scripture Texts

Since the children have learned something about the Bible in the first lesson, they should be encouraged to memorize the simpler Scripture texts and, when occasion presents itself at any time of the day, the week, or the year, to apply them to particular situations spontaneously. For example: It is spring. The first gentle rain and long-desired shower arrives. Everybody gives a sigh of gratitude and relief. How much better understood at such a time will be the words referring to the coming of the Redeemer: "He shall come down . . ." (p. 182).

The Problems of Everyday Life

The problems are primarily intended to set the pupils thinking about their own actions. Nevertheless, it is wiser for the teacher not to make the application directly in every case. Also, she must be careful to direct attention to the case in hand rather than to the "right answer" which the pupils too often try to read from her face. A great deal of sympathy, skill, and tact are required for this phase of the work. Pupils should be commended for their efforts to solve the problem, even if they do not give the right answer. Under no circumstances should the class be allowed to laugh at one another's mistakes or make exclamations of surprise or reproach. *The positive good should always be stressed in preference to the negative evil.*

Interesting Things to Do

The extra activities suggested furnish assimilative material that is more valuable than may appear at first sight. Learning is a slow process, especially with young children. The "things to do" give them a chance for repetition and review of the lesson without danger of monotony. Take, for example, a sand-table project of Noe and the Ark. In order to build the project, the children must refer to the story again and again. They talk about it with their teacher, their classmates, their parents. They repeat the story to other teachers and children who visit the room and tell about every detail connected with the project; and all this with great eagerness and pleasure. Surely, the story and truths underlying the lesson have impressed themselves more deeply than by the old-time repetition and drill method. Besides, the children have had a chance to exercise their ingenuity, to go out to look for suitable material, to learn the names of animals, etc. And they have had a valuable lesson in co-operation.

It is especially in activities of this kind, however, that the teacher must be careful not to lose sight of the *end* for which she is striving. After all, it is not the success of the project itself that counts, nor the variety of animals obtained, nor the splendid showing the class makes before visitors. It is, rather, the deepening of the lesson itself and the truths underlying it, that has permanent value for the religion class.

It need hardly be pointed out how well these different activities may be fitted into other class periods, depending on their nature. The art work may be done during the art period, the language work during the language period, and so on. The teacher must not, however, make special and strained effort to bring religion into every hour of the day. Rather, all subjects should correlate naturally with one another and religious thought and principle should permeate all.

It is understood that the work, no matter of what nature, be always in keeping with the dignity and sublimity of the subject matter.

Good Things to Read

If possible the supplementary readers should be placed on a shelf accessible to the pupils at any time. A small table with chairs around it placed in a corner of the room to suggest a reading atmosphere, would be helpful. Pupils should be free to refer to the books during their spare moments and so have ready for use some of the stories or poems mentioned in their text.

Do not neglect the reading list. The stories and poems listed always have some bearing on the lesson. Other stories and selections may be substituted or added by the pupils. The important thing again is to help along the main thought of the lesson, to enrich and broaden the children's knowledge.

Doctrine

The questions referring to the doctrine serve mostly as a review of the truths the children have already learned in the first three grades. The teacher is free to add as many others as she desires. Too much must not be made of formal memorization of definite answers. Principally, children must learn to *live* their religion. Every lesson in the book aims specifically at bringing about this result. It is foolish to believe that the memorized lines of doctrine will of themselves make good Catholics of pupils. It is the spirit that counts.

Since some instructors may require memory work of the pupils, however, answers to the questions in the text, are added in the manual. The *Baltimore Catechism* may be used as a guide, if desired. It may be well to note here what Father Drinkwater says in this connection in his Introduction to Tahon's *The First Instruction of Children and Beginners,* pages 18 and 19.

"It is asserted that without a fixed form of words, teachers, whether good or bad, will just flounder about vaguely, with no pegs on which to hang their doctrine, so that the children in the end will retain nothing definite at all. This is quite true, of course, but it is not a reason for teaching the answers of the Catechism to young children; it is only a reason why the teacher should often crystallize his teaching into little fixed phrases and sentences which the children will take in and remember."

Poems, Hymns, Quotations, Pictures

The teacher should make it a point to collect suitable poems, hymns, quotations, pictures, and other material for use in her religion class. A separate envelope or file for the material referring to each lesson would simplify the teacher's daily preparation for another year. Some of the simpler poems should be memorized, others should be read by the teacher for appreciation. Sometimes, as has already been mentioned, a poem, hymn, or picture may be used to introduce the day's lesson and arouse new interest and attention. The worth-while selections and songs learned by the class should be frequently repeated. At times some of them may be gathered into an impromptu program for some special feast day. The children will get a great deal of pleasure in taking turns to select the numbers for the program all by themselves. Not all selections, hymns, or pictures need necessarily be of a specifically religious nature. "Religion is life."

The children should be allowed to sing much and often. Preferably such hymns should be selected as are simple, dignified, and devotional. They, too, should be correlated with every other subject and used freely at any time that they best serve their purpose. For example, the teacher may have impressed the lesson of faith, hope, and love, upon the pupils. They might most fittingly sing, then, a hymn containing these acts.

Pictures should also be used freely. At times a picture to be used in introducing a lesson may be put up some days ahead of time so that interest may be aroused and comments and questions exchanged.

Liturgy

The liturgy in its simplest form should go hand in hand with the daily religion lesson. The teacher should, above all, train the children to hear Mass with attention and devotion. They should know that they attend Mass to unite themselves with the priest at the altar, in offering the Great Sacrifice. They should, therefore, be encouraged to watch the actions of the priest and learn more and more about their meaning.

The feasts of the Liturgical Year should be called to their attention and simply explained. Again the teacher must keep in mind that it is the spirit that counts, the *living* with Mother Church, and not a mere knowledge of the facts.

Lesson 10 offers special opportunity to learn more about the Mass. A good, simple book, such as *The Best Gift,* by Gales, which follows the liturgical thought of the Mass, will serve as a splendid guide (see general references).

First Holy Communion

Book III in the Highway to Heaven Series, *The Life of the Soul* is intended to prepare the children for their First Holy

Communion. Also, there is brief study of the Mass in Preparation for Holy Communion in the *First Grade Teacher's Manual*. It is followed by a unit on First Holy Communion, both being intended for pupils in any of the lower grades.

It is assumed that children of the fourth year have already received their First Holy Communion. However, should they not have done so, the religion work for this year may be readily adapted for this purpose. Instruction for First Holy Communion should properly be introduced through a study of the Mass. Lesson 10 prepares the way; Lesson 11 may be studied more at length by way of preparation. A Mass Booklet followed up by a Communion Booklet could be made by each child in the course of the year. Future lessons in the text can each be made to yield their share in contributing to the children's preparation. The longing for the Redeemer by the people of the Old Testament should be closely associated with their own longing to receive the same Redeemer into their hearts.

Creative Work

The teacher should encourage the children to self-expression whenever possible. Plays, stories, poems, drawings, posters, etc., will all become more valuable in proportion to the child's own participation in and personal contribution to the activity. Direction will be necessary to some extent, especially at first, but the teacher should always keep in mind that child activity is preferable to teacher activity when working out the assimilative material that is suggested in connection with the lessons. Let it be kept in mind, however, that all work connected with the teaching of religion must give evidence of the reverence due so holy a subject.

Teacher's References

If daily, careful preparation is necessary for the teacher in other branches, how much more so in all-important subject of religion. This manual is planned to give every possible aid. It offers suggestions of the presentation and development of every lesson in the book. In addition it lists a number of references for the enrichment of the teacher's own knowledge. The teacher should, above all, read directly from the Holy Bible, the passages from which the stories in the text are taken. There she will gather first-hand information and inspiration for her work. The many problems that present themselves in the Old Testament are adequately dealt with in *Biblical Questions* (Bandas). Needless to say, they are largely explanations for the teacher and not for the pupils. Other references should also be consulted, not necessarily only those which are mentioned in this manual (see list of references, p. 170).

Teacher's Notes

In the space left for the teacher's notes, questions such as the following should be answered:

Is the period of time suggested for this lesson too long or too short?

What poems, pictures, hymns, stories, etc., have proved most interesting and helpful, and where can I find them?

What changes do I desire to make in the work next year?

Is there any criticism of the text? What?

Are there any other points I should like to remember for next year?

If necessary, an extra blank page may be pasted into the manual for these notes. They are intended as a reference for another year and a consequent improved presentation.

RELIGION COURSE — GRADE FOUR

The Plan Outlined

The lessons are arranged according to Biblical topics. To these are added (in parentheses) other topics that have been developed from the story. Different phases of the subject may be treated according to the needs of the class and the preference of the Reverend Instructor. They must, however, always have a close bearing upon the lesson of the week.

SEPTEMBER

First Week — Lesson   1. The Holy Bible
  2. How God Made the World
    (God, the Creator of heaven and earth)*

Second Week — Lesson   3. God's Garden on Earth
  4. The Sin of God's People
  5. God's Wonderful Promise
    (Man, a creature composed of body and soul)

Third Week — Lesson   6. Cain Becomes a Wanderer
    (The sin of Cain; or
    The necessity of controlling our thoughts and actions; or
    Jealousy, hatred, etc., and their evil effects)

Fourth Week — Lesson   7. Rain for Forty Days
  8. A Rainbow in the Sky
    (Faith, hope, and love, the worship we owe to God.
    Sacrifices of the Old Law, their

---

*These discussions must always grow out of the lesson and re-enforce its facts and motives.

12

significance, their application to the Mass. To be continued next week)

OCTOBER

First Week — Lesson 9. The Land of Promise
10. A Priest of the Most High God (The Mass, taught preferably as a whole at this time)

Second Week — Lesson 11. Three Guests Come to Abraham (Holy Communion, taught as an integral part of the Mass)

Third Week — Lesson 12. The End of Two Cities
13. Abraham Obeys God's Voice (The evil of sin — see next week. True sorrow for sin. Jesus Christ, the Second Person of the Blessed Trinity)

Fourth Week — Lesson 14. Rebecca at the Well
15. Esau Sells His Birthright
16. The Hunter Returns (Mortal and venial sin. The power of prayer)

NOVEMBER

First Week — Lesson 17. A Dream of God
18. Jacob Meets Rachel (The Church. Christ's presence in the Blessed Sacrament — Behavior in church)

Second Week — Lesson 19. Forgiveness (Temporal and eternal punishment due to sin — "Forgive us our trespasses . . .")

Third Week — Lesson 20. Joseph, the Dreamer (Obedience to parents)

Fourth Week — Lesson 21. Sold as a Slave (Purity)

Fifth Week — Lesson 22. The Forgotten Prisoner
23. Go to Joseph
(God's Providence)

DECEMBER
First Week — Lesson 24. The Famine Comes to Chanaan
25. Back Again to Egypt
(Gratitude for and care of
God's gifts)

Second Week — Lesson 26. The Missing Cup
27. The Return of Good for Evil
28. A Father Finds His Long-Lost
Son
(Joseph a type of Jesus.
Love of enemy)

Third Week — Lesson 29. Jacob Blesses His Children
30. A Man Whom God Loved
(The Resurrection of the Body)

JANUARY
First Week — Lesson 31. A Princess Finds an Infant Boy
(A Mother's love, type of Mary's
love for us.
Devotion to Mary)

Second Week — Lesson 32. Called by God
(Sacramentals in general or some
few sacramentals in particular)

Third Week — Lesson 33. Egypt is Punished with Plagues
(The sacraments in general.
Holy orders and matrimony in
particular. Other sacraments are
touched upon later)

Fourth Week — Lesson 34. Walking Through the Red Sea
(Confirmation, the sacrament that
makes us strong to fight for the
honor of God)

FEBRUARY
First Week — Lesson 35. God Sends Food from Heaven

36. God Gives the Ten Commandments
(The Ten Commandments. Continued next week)

Second Week — Lesson 37. The Israelites Worship a Golden Calf
(The Ten Commandments continued)

Third Week — Lesson 38. Scouting in the Land of Promise
(The Ten Commandments, stressing particularly the eighth)

Fourth Week — Lesson 39. Water from a Rock

40. The Death of a Great Leader
(The Apostles' Creed)

MARCH

First Week — Lesson 41. Back in the Land of Promise

42. Gedeon, the First of the Judges
(Baptism. The effects of Baptism)

Second Week — Lesson 43. A Faithful Daughter

44. The Lord Speaks to a Child
(Sunday, a day of rest — how to keep it holy.
The examination of conscience)

Third Week — Lesson 45. The First King of Israel
(Obedience to authority, particularly to civil authority)

APRIL

First Week — Lesson 46. A Shepherd Boy Becomes King

47. David Kills a Giant

48. David Sings of the Redeemer
(The Psalms as prayers of the Church.
Kindness to the poor, the sick, the unfortunate)

Second Week — Lesson 49. A King Who Asked for Wisdom

UNIT I

GOD'S BEAUTIFUL, WONDERFUL WORLD

Time: Four weeks in September.

Feasts to Remember

Teach the children to live with Mother Church by suggesting in a simple way the spirit of the Church in the various seasons and by keeping them in close touch with the feasts of the year. A few words about the feast of the day, the first thing in the morning, will suffice. Have the pupils find what color of vestment is worn and why. Note the suggestions for some of the following days.

September 8, Nativity of the Blessed Virgin Mary
(The birthday of the Mother of the Redeemer. Sing a hymn in honor of Mary today.)

12, Holy Name of Mary
(See poem in the textbook, p. 111.)

15, The Seven Sorrows of the Blessed Virgin Mary
(Have a picture of the sorrowful Mother posted and under it the words of Jeremias: "O all you that pass by the way, attend and see, if there be any sorrow like to my sorrow." Text, p. 213.)
Ember Days

21, St. Matthew, Apostle and Evangelist
(Have the children look for a text from the Gospel of St. Matthew in the Holy Bible, for example: Matt. v. 1–16.)

24, Our Lady of Mercy
(Sing a hymn in honor of Our Lady.)

26, St. Isaac Jogues and Companions, Martyrs
(Catholic readers relate the story. Read it to the class.)

17

29, St. Michael, Archangel

30, St. Jerome, Priest, Confessor, Doctor

Introducing the Textbook to the Children

Before Christ Came is a religion book and should therefore be treated with a reverence due to all religious objects. A little talk to the class before the books are given out, or when you are ready to start the first lesson, will help a great deal to create the right attitude.

The book tells about God. The stories are retold from the Holy Bible, the greatest book that was ever written. We should, therefore, think more of this book than of any other. When we think much of a person or thing we are very careful how we act toward it.

Look at the cover and talk about the symbols. In the upper left-hand corner we have the symbol of God the Creator, the First Person of the Blessed Trinity. Our book tells us of the creation of the world. In the right-hand corner is the symbol of the fall of man, about which we shall also read in our book. In the lower left-hand corner is the symbol of the Mystical Rose, the Virgin Mother of the Redeemer, who was promised in paradise after the fall of man. In the lower right-hand corner is the star foretold by the Prophet, which announced the birth of the Redeemer. The central figure shows the Highway to Heaven. The road is narrow and steep, but with the help which God gives us, we can reach the summit safely.

Much will depend upon your own attitude as you approach the lessons with your pupils.

With the pupils read the editor's letter and discuss the suggestions made in it.

INTRODUCTORY PARAGRAPH

God's Beautiful, Wonderful World

The introduction to each unit should be read either by the teacher or the pupils. It is intended to make the pupils see each unit as a whole first, and also to tie up the stories that follow with those that have gone before.

After the eight stories of the first unit have been read, return to this introduction and read it again. See whether the pupils have a full grasp of the unit by asking questions such as the following:

How did God make this beautiful, wonderful world of ours?

Who were the first people that lived in it?

Name all the people that you have read about so far.

How did God show that He loved His people even after they had sinned?

What was the wonderful promise that He made?

Lessons 1 and 2

First Week in September

Aim: The first lesson aims to give the pupils a clear idea of what the Holy Bible is and why we should love and revere it.

Preparation: Have one or more good copies of the Holy Bible in the classroom so that all can see the book and handle it.

Read Lesson 1

Explain that the Holy Bible was originally written in Hebrew and Greek but that it has been translated into all languages so that everybody might read it.

In a simple way also make the children understand that, since the Bible is the Word of God, the Church is very careful not to have anybody change any part of it. The English Bible approved by the Catholic Church is usually called the "Douay Version" because the Old Testament was first published by the English College at Douay in the year 1609.

A Bible History, such as this, is not the Holy Bible itself but contains some of the more important stories of the Bible, retold in a way easy for children to read and understand. Of course, it is much better to read the Word of God directly from the Holy Bible.

Try to awaken in the children a great desire to hear and know more about the Word of God as contained in the Bible. With this desire awakened, the simple Scripture texts to be memorized in the course of the year will take on new value and meaning.

When a religion book has been written by a Catholic, it is first read by some learned priest appointed by the bishop, to make sure that there has been no error about any teaching of the Church. If the priest finds that the words of the book are according to the teachings of the Church, he writes the words *Nihil obstat* (nothing hinders the publication) and signs his name under them. That is a sign to all Catholics that whatever the book says about matters of faith and morals (what we must believe and what we must do to be saved) is true. Then the bishop or archbishop also signs his name and writes the word *Imprimatur,* which means, "It may be printed."

Why is the Church so careful about the Holy Bible and other religious books? Because sometimes people write books which teach false doctrines. When others read such books, they drink in these false teachings like poison. A good Catholic, therefore, makes sure that any book about religion which he reads has been approved by the Church; that is, that it has the *Imprimatur* of the archbishop or bishop on it.

Now have the pupils look on the inside of the title page for the *Nihil obstat* and *Imprimatur.*

Also have them look into other books to see whether they have been approved by the Church. Why does their Arithmetic not have these words? It does not deal with the teaching of religion. Their prayer books will have an *Imprimatur* also.

Now Answer the Following Questions:

The questions following each lesson are intended to test the comprehension of the pupils. They may be used for oral or silent work.

If necessary the lesson should be read a second time for a fuller appreciation of the content.

Interesting Things to Do:

1. If you have a Holy Bible at home, see whether you can find the *Imprimatur.*

2. In the Holy Bible find how far the Old Testament reaches and what part is the New Testament.

3. The very first book of the Holy Bible is the Book of Genesis. Find it.

4. See whether you can find the following books in the Holy Bible: Psalms, Job, Daniel, Numbers, St. John, St. Luke, St. Matthew, St. Mark. Which of these belong to the Old Testament and which to the New?

5. See whether you can find other religion books that have the *Imprimatur*.

Teacher's References:

The teacher should make every effort to be well prepared for her religious instruction. She should not be satisfied, however, with information she is to impart to the pupils but enrich her own store of knowledge to the best of her ability. A number of references are added after each lesson to indicate some of the valuable material at her disposal. The list is by no means complete. Other readings may be substituted when these are not available.

Encyclical of Pope Leo XIII on the Study of Holy Scripture (sometimes used as an introduction to the Holy Bible).

Bandas, *Biblical Questions*, Introductory, pp. 11–20.

Catholic School Journal, "The Book of Books," Bandas, Oct., 1933.

Laux, *Introduction to the Bible,* pp. 1–22.

Catholic Encyclopedia, see "Imprimatur," "Censor of Books."

Lesson 2

Aim: This lesson aims to teach the children how the world was created by God and what it means to be a creature of God and belong to Him entirely. It should also give the pupils a fuller appreciation of all creatures as gifts of God to man.

Preparation: Plan an interesting way of introducing this lesson. Since the story of the creation is most likely already well known to the children, the lesson might be read as the last thing, more for an appreciation of the simple, beautiful language of the Bible, and as a summary of the week's work and discussion. In that case develop the lesson on Creation by asking questions such as those on page 7, and carry out the other activities that are suggested.

Explain that the word *day* does not here mean 24 hours, but rather a long period of time, possibly thousands of years.

Give the children a clear notion of the meaning of *Creator, create,* and *creature.*

Creator: God, who made all things by an act of His will.[1]

Create: To give life to a thing or cause something to be, by an act of the will.

Creature: That which has been created by God and therefore belongs to Him.

Explain also the following words:

Firmament: The sky.

Increase and multiply: To become more and more in numbers.

Image and likeness: Explain simply that the likeness of man to God is in the soul and not in the body.

Read Lesson 2 yourself first and try to sense the dignity and simplicity of the Biblical language which has been retained as far as possible in the story. As suggested, have the pupils read the story at the end of the week's work.

Using Good Judgment:

Aim to make the pupils understand the proper motive for doing the right thing. God sees and knows all things. A good Catholic boy or girl realizes this truth and therefore needs no other watchman to see that he does right. He does it because God wants it so. Making the right choice is not enough. The children must also desire to act accordingly. Just to give the answer that the teacher expects is not sufficient. Create the right attitude and strive so to influence the heart and the will that right action will follow right choice. Whenever possible the

---

[1]Teachers will find the *Thorndike Century Junior Dictionary* (Scott, Foresman & Co.) helpful in the explanations of the meanings of words. — Ed.

children should be given an opportunity to practice in some small way what they have recognized as being the right thing to do.

Speak of some of the beautiful things God has given us for our enjoyment and try to make the pupils see how wrong it is willfully to destroy or harm God's gifts of trees, flowers, birds, lawns, etc.

How to Make a Character Book:

A simple loose-leaf notebook may be used, if desired. The plan should be varied from time to time. That is the advantage of having just a few sheets at a time. The book can then be taken home after several weeks and another (perhaps under another name) can take its place without much work or trouble.

Topics for Discussion:

Discuss each of the sentences and selections individually. Direct the pupils to choose just one or the other which will be most useful. It will be necessary at first to assist the children in their choice and to make them understand how desirable it is to conquer one's own faults. It is better to concentrate on one single point than to plan on doing too much at once.

Call attention at this time to the beauties of nature, especially to the change in the color of foliage. From nature lead to nature's God, but in a simple, natural way, without strain or effort. Stevenson's quotation should be memorized and used occasionally at sight of a beautiful scene, a flower, or a bird.

More Things for You to Do:

1. These posters can be made very easily and will help the children appreciate God's gifts. Post them in the classroom and refer to them occasionally, for example, during the oral or written language work. In this way the thought of God will be associated with various activities and impress itself more deeply upon the child's mind. Note what Dr. Shields says in this connection in his *Primary Methods:* "The fatuous policy that is sometimes followed in Catholic schools, of copying the curriculum of the de-Christianized schools, and adding to this

a half hour religious instruction each day, can scarcely fail to destroy effectively the roots of Catholic faith in the lives of children entrusted to these schools by confiding parents."

2 and 3. Naturally not all these activities need be carried out if there is lack of time.

4. An occasion to bring out individual effort and initiative. Have your books in a place easily accessible to the children at any time.

5. The aim of this exercise is to repeat some of the thoughts and words of the lesson, to add interest, and furnish purposeful activity.

6. Ask questions to recall the thoughts developed about the Holy Bible so that the children will appreciate the quotation more fully.

7. This exercise offers an occasion to review the Apostles' Creed. The aim of the frequent references to familiar prayers is to give a better understanding and fuller appreciation of these prayers which the children only too frequently recite mechanically.

Read or let one of the children read the first part of the Book of Genesis and compare it with the story in their own books.

Can You Answer These Questions?

In this grade as all through grades 1, 2, and 3, doctrinal truths have been learned naturally and simply, step by step, with the story. The questions at the end of the lesson merely summarize what has been learned during the week, not as memorized facts, but as an outgrowth of the thoughts developed in the story and other activities. Learning these answers from memory is not religion in itself. Unless the truths which the child has learned become assimilated and are carried out in daily life, memorized facts remain cold and fruitless. Assimilative material is furnished by means of the various activities that aim to impress religious principles. The questions repeat the truths already learned, in compact form, to assist the memory. If the pupils have mastered the answers satisfactorily and intelligently, there is no further need for mechanical memorization unless it is required by the instructor.

The following are the answers to the questions asked in the text:

1. God made the world.
2. God is the Creator of heaven and earth and all things.
3. God had no beginning and will have no end.
4. God made me.
5. God made me to know Him, to love Him, and to serve Him here on earth and to be happy with Him forever in heaven.
6. I can show that I love God by obeying His commandments, by prayer, and by good works, etc.
7. I can serve God by doing good to all His creatures, especially to men who are made according to His image and likeness.
8. God is everywhere.
9. We cannot see God because He is a pure spirit and has no body.

Teacher's References:

The Holy Bible, Gen. i.

Biblical Questions, "The Six Days," pp. 55–59.

Teacher's Handbook to Bible History, "Creation of the World," pp. 5–8.

Catholic Action Series, Book I, "God's Image," pp. 69–71.

Teacher's Notes:

(See page 11.)

Lessons 3, 4, and 5

Second Week in September

Aim: To show how sin entered into the world through our first parents by disobedience to God's law, and how it came about that God promised a Redeemer.

Preparation: Words to be explained:

Knowledge: What one knows. When we can understand something clearly, we say we have a knowledge of it. *Serpent,* a big snake. *Evil,* wicked, bad. *Cursed,* the earth was cursed; that is, it was filled with sorrow and trouble and evil of all kinds, on account of sin.

Show whatever pictures you can, referring to Adam and Eve and the garden of Paradise.

Read Lesson 3

Explain simply any passage that may not be clear to the children. Talk about the lesson, especially about the beauty of the garden, Adam's loneliness, and God's goodness in sending him a companion.

Read Lesson 4

Dwell especially on temptation. Before sin is committed the evil spirit pictures everything to us as being good and able to make us happy. Afterwards everything looks quite different. Let the children show how this happened in the case of Adam and Eve.

Read Lesson 5

Explain simply, the words: "I will put enmities between thee and the woman, between thy seed and her seed." On this wonderful promise are based all the stories of the Old Testament. Keep it always before the minds of the pupils.

God has given us His commandments, as we shall see later. To refuse to keep His commandments is to commit sin.

"Dust you are and into dust you shall return" is still used by the Church to remind us that our bodies will one day return to dust. Explain when and how these words are now used. Return to the lesson again on Ash Wednesday.

Using Good Judgment:

1. Point out that while we are obliged by the Church to go to Mass on Sundays and holydays of obligation, a good Catholic child who knows the great value of the Mass, will go chiefly because he wishes to praise, honor, and thank God, and not because he *has* to go.

2. Bonnie's orders are to stay at home and she must obey. Discuss this problem fully. Bonnie's mother has good reasons for giving the orders. When God gives us a law, we must obey. He knows what is best for us. Our parents take the place of God. Good laws are not made just to be kept. There is always a good reason behind them although we may not see it. Have the children show what might happen if Bonnie does not stay with the baby.

3. This question is intended merely to give the children a chance to think and talk about the matter. It should be the teacher's constant aim to direct the children to do their own thinking.

More Things for You to Do:

1. This little dramatization should be carried out if at all possible. Let Adam and Eve take turns in telling the story of Paradise. Occasionally the children interrupt with a question.

Most of all, Adam impresses upon them the fact that some day the promise will be fulfilled. They must watch and pray. They must make themselves worthy of His Presence by leading good lives. They must also tell their children about it, so that, if He has not yet come, they, too, will watch for Him.

2, 3, and 4. These activities will have value only if the story is constantly repeated with them.

5. Be sure to dwell on the meaning of this quotation (not minutely) and to review it occasionally.

6. This should be an outgrowth of the discussion on the temptation of Eve. The tempter acts the same with us. Therefore we must be on our guard. We must, above all, pray for help and strength.

7. These stories may be used as oral or written language work.

Can You Answer These Questions?

1. Man is composed of body and soul.

2. Our first parents were Adam and Eve.

3. Adam and Eve were punished because they disobeyed God and ate of the forbidden fruit.

4. Sin is any willful thought, word, act, or omission against the law of God. The word *willful* means "done on purpose"; the word *omission* means "not doing what we are expected to do."

5. Heaven was closed until the Redeemer came to earth to open it again for us.

Teacher's References:

The Holy Bible, Gen. iii, iv.

Biblical Questions, "The Fall," "The Fall and Science," "Death and Science," etc., pp. 92–112.

Teacher's Handbook to Bible History, "Creation of Man," "Paradise," pp. 8–10.

Catholic Action Series, Book I, "Consequence of the Fall," pp. 72–75.

Teacher's Notes:

Lesson 6

Third Week in September

Aim: To show, through the story of Cain and Abel, the result of the Fall of Man on human nature; also the importance of self-control in our own lives and the evil of giving way to jealousy and hate.

Preparation: Words to be explained:

Sacrifice: In the Old Testament people offered fruits or animals to God by destroying or burning them, to show that

God alone and no one else was the owner; that was called sacrifice.

Jealous: To be sad or angry because someone else is praised or seems to have more or better things than we.

Control: To have in one's power; to hold on to our feelings and not to let them get away from us.

Desires: Wishes and longings for the things we do not have.

In this and future lessons recall by means of a few review questions what has gone before, in order to establish a connection. The questions may be somewhat as follows:

Where did Adam and Eve live before they sinned?

Did they always remain in Paradise?

Why were they punished?

How were they punished?

What great Promise did God make to them?

Do you think Adam and Eve were ever as happy after they left Paradise as before?

Practical Application

In the suggestions for self-control, lead the children to do a little thinking for themselves. Follow up each statement with actual cases from the children's own experiences. Forming right attitudes is teaching the children to live in accordance with God's plans. It is religion lived and not merely stored in the memory. Make sure, therefore, that the statements are not merely read but that they call attention to the right thing to do in specific cases and particularly in the children's own lives.

What Would You Do?

1. Do not be satisfied with a mere "Yes" or "No" in answer to these questions. Make the pupils feel that they are expected to help solve the problem. Be specific in suggesting remedies. For example: Charles has thoughts of jealousy in his mind. As soon as he notices them he should say to himself: "That is jealousy. I ought to be ashamed of myself. How would I like to have others feel that way about me when I am praised? I should be glad for John. Dear Jesus, help me forget such thoughts. I will tell John that I think he had a good lesson and that I am glad for him."

2. Ordinarily the best thing to do would be to talk to Dan about it and tell him how wrong it is to accept a prize which he did not deserve. Here is a chance to point out the difference between tattling and telling what ought to be told in the right place.

3. Watch for just such little cases in school and on the playground and then apply the lesson directly. Show what a splendid thing it is to be a good loser.

4. Talk this problem over and see whether you can make the lesson sink in.

5. Explain that self-control does not necessarily mean giving in to everybody at all times. There are times when a child has a right to stand firm. Still he can control himself by not losing his temper or striking back.

6. Will should take his disappointment bravely. It will help him to become a brave, splendid boy.

7. Show how we must learn to control our likes and dislikes and how we can at the same time do little acts of kindness for the love of God.

8. Take each of the three points and show the possible results for Tom.

More Things for You to Do:

These early altars may, perhaps, have been crude elevations or piles of stone. Let the children work out their own ideas, however.

Can You Answer These Questions?

1. Cain should have put away his evil thoughts.

2. Cain committed the sin of murder.

3. Yes, Cain's sin could have been forgiven if he had been truly sorry and asked God's forgiveness.

4. Cain did not ask God to forgive him.

5. Our mortal sins can be forgiven by a good confession or, if there is no chance to go to confession, by an act of perfect contrition, joined with the wish to receive the sacrament of penance.

Add other questions if desired.

Teacher's References:

The Holy Bible, Gen. iv.

Teacher's Handbook to Bible History, "Cain and Abel," pp. 13–15.

Catholic Action Series, Book II, Chap. XXI, "Thou shalt not kill."

Teacher's Notes:

Lessons 7 and 8

Fourth Week in September

Aim: Lessons 7 and 8 aim to show, on the one hand, how God cared for Noe and his family and saved them from the great flood because they loved and served Him; and, on the other hand, how God hates sin and how He punishes those who offend Him.

Preparation: Read over both lessons and decide on the activities of the week. Some of them fit very well into other periods of the day, as a glance at "Interesting Things to Do" will show. For example, the poems may be used during the reading or language class, the rainbow colors may be studied during the art class, the names of animals are added to the spelling list, etc. Here, as throughout the book, the aim is to make religious thought lend itself naturally to any and every subject in the curriculum. At no time should there be an attempt made to force a thought or subject into a place where it cannot be developed naturally.

The following words may require some explanation:

Destroy: To put an end to. If I were to take your book away from you, tear it to bits, and throw the pieces into the wastebasket, you would say that I destroyed your book; that is, I put an end to it. Now will one of you please destroy this paper? Can this school building be destroyed? How? etc.

Flood: To fill to overflowing. When the water of a river flows over its banks and fills the land around it, we say there is a flood. *The Flood* means the water that covered the earth in the time of Noe.

Pitch: Boiled tar.

Raven: A large black bird, like a crow.

Olive branch: A twig from the olive tree.

Despise: To look down on someone (give examples).

Forsake: To leave behind, to go away from someone. Children forsake their parents if they never trouble to help or support them. We forsake God when we harden our hearts and do not listen to His teachings.

If possible have on hand a picture of the Deluge to show to the children. There should also be several Bible Histories in the classroom for supplementary reading so that pupils may read other versions of the story. The teacher herself should read the account from the Holy Bible and perhaps also read a short selection of it for the children.

Now Read and Discuss Lesson 7

The introductory paragraph serves to make a connection between the foregoing stories and those to be studied this week. Aim to keep this connection before the pupils.

The faithful Noe and his family were the only ones saved from the flood. Noe's family, therefore, was the only one from whom the Redeemer might be expected. What a wonderful reward for his faith, and hope, and love!

We can imagine the family in the ark sitting together and talking. Perhaps Noe is telling his children's children once again about Paradise, the sin of Adam, their forefather, and the promise of the Redeemer. We can hear him admonishing them always to remain faithful to God, who is even now saving them from the flood; to believe in Him, to hope in Him, and to love Him.

Let the children talk about the picture on page 24. We can imagine the wicked people standing around and laughing at Noe for going into the ark when there is no sign of rain. The same thing happens today. There are people who laugh at us because we get up early Sunday mornings to go to Mass, or because we do not eat meat on Fridays. Like Noe, we shall let them laugh. Some day, perhaps very soon, they will find out who was right. God does not always punish at once. But God always punishes evil and rewards good. We shall see all that clearly when it comes to the Last Judgment. We shall see it often, too, as we read the lessons in this book.

Picture the waters of the flood rising higher and higher. The wicked people climb up on the highest rocks. We can guess how they feel when they remember making fun of Noe, who listened to the voice of God. Now he is safe in the ark and they must die in the flood. God is wiping out the terrible shame of their sin. The waters rise higher and higher; at last the people are covered over by the flood. What a terrible thing sin must be in the eyes of God.

Now Read and Discuss Lesson 8

Do not overlook the thought questions that suggest themselves in the various lessons. Here we have questions such as the following:

What did the warm wind do for the earth?

Why did Noe wait forty days before he opened the window?

What did Noe find out from the dove that returned with an olive branch?

Noe showed his faith by doing as God wished, without question or doubt. He showed his hope by trusting in God to save him and his family from the flood. He showed his love and gratitude by offering sacrifice to God for all His goodness and by serving Him faithfully.

A review of the acts of faith, hope, and charity at this time will help the children to say these prayers with more understanding and devotion.

Interesting Things to Do:

1. This may be an opportune time to teach the children an appreciation of Rain Poems such as may be found in *Child Story Readers*, Book IV. The language or reading period should be used for the work, but the children should quite naturally recall the rain that lasted forty days and forty nights.

2. A few words about gratitude may be in place here. Keep in mind throughout the year's work that it is not so much the finding of the quotation that counts, as the fact that, in looking for it, and in entering it into his book, the pupil is reminded of his own obligation to show gratitude to God and to his neighbor for benefits received. In other words, the teacher must continually strive to stress our dependence on God and the necessity of carrying out in our lives, the lessons learned in school.

3. In the dramatization bring out the underlying thought developed during the discussion of the lesson.

4. The story itself should often be repeated during the project. The project is only a means, remember, to impress the children with the story and its deep significance.

5. For suggestions see *Art Education Through Religion,* references page 170.

6. Add the names of animals to your spelling list.

7. Talk over the quotations with the pupils and then let each one choose the quotation he prefers. Point out that often young people refuse to listen to the advice of their parents, teachers, or priests and then find out too late that, after all, older people know better when they advise us for our own good.

Use the quotations again, in future activities, as in dramatizations. A playlet involving obedience to parents, or advice from elders, would call for quotations of this kind.

If the pupils have become interested in looking for passages from the Bible, let them have the pleasure of finding quotations from time to time, especially those that are mentioned in their texts.

Can You Answer These Questions?

1. Noe knew that God cannot tell a lie. God is perfect. He cannot deceive nor be deceived. (Refer to Act of Faith.)

2. God is all powerful; that is, He can do all things. Nothing is hard for Him. (If the teacher finds it necessary, she may review all the attributes of God at this time. God is perfect. He has no beginning and no end. He is everywhere. He sees all things. He knows all things. He can do all things. He is just, holy, and merciful. We cannot see Him because He is a spirit.)

3. Noe offered sacrifice by taking some of the animals and burning them on an altar. In this way he wished to acknowledge that all things belong to Him alone, that God is the Creator and Lord of all things, who has a right over life and death.

4. We offer sacrifice through the Holy Mass. In the Holy Mass Christ Himself is offered for us. We can see how much greater is this sacrifice than that of animals. We, too, can offer

sacrifice to God, then, by offering Christ in the Mass, in order to praise, adore, petition, and thank God the Father. How rich we are, to have Jesus offer Himself for us at Mass. How we should love to go to Mass often, in order to show God our love, our faith, our hope, and our gratitude.

5. The Mass is the unbloody sacrifice of the body and blood of Christ. The bloody sacrifice took place when Jesus died on Mt. Calvary.

6. A Catholic must go to Mass every Sunday and holyday of obligation. However, a Catholic who understands the great value of the Mass will go as often as he can, on weekdays, too. He will consider going to Mass a great privilege rather than a duty.

7. A Catholic should keep the Sunday holy. (Discuss what might be done.) He should not do hard labor. (Call for examples.)

Teacher's References:

The Holy Bible, Gen. vi–viii.

Biblical Questions, "The Deluge and the Ark," pp. 115–120.

Teacher's Handbook to Bible History, "The Deluge," pp. 16–19.

Teacher's Notes:

Test for Unit I

Twenty Points is a Perfect Score

1. The most wonderful book that was ever written is the ......(Holy Bible).......

2. God made two great lights: The ......(sun)...... to rule the day, and the ......(moon)...... to rule the night.

3. Last of all God made the first ......(man)...... and the first ......(woman).......

4. God put Adam into a beautiful garden called ...... (Paradise).......

5. The first woman was named ......(Eve)...... which means, "Mother of all the living."

6. God said: "If you eat of the tree of the knowledge of good and evil, you shall ......(die)......."

7. But the serpent said: "No, you shall not die, but your eyes shall be opened, and you shall be as ......(God)......."

8. Eve told God that the ......(serpent)...... deceived her.

9. Because ......(Adam)...... and ......(Eve)...... ate of the forbidden fruit, they were sent out of Paradise.

10. Two sons of Adam and Eve were ......(Cain)...... and ......(Abel).......

11. God told ......(Noe)...... to build an ark.

12. When the ark was finished God sent a ......(rain-flood) ...... which lasted forty days and forty nights.

13. Noe took with him into the ark his family and a pair of every kind of ......(animal).......

14. After the flood Noe built an altar and offered ...... (sacrifice)...... to God.

15. God promised that He would never again destroy man by sending a ......(flood)...... and as a sign of His promise, He placed a ......(rainbow)...... in the sky.

UNIT II

THREE LEADERS OF GOD'S PEOPLE

Time: Four weeks in October.

Feasts to Remember

October 2, Holy Guardian Angels
3, Little Flower of Jesus
4, St. Francis of Assisi
7, Holy Rosary
15, St. Teresa
18, St. Luke
(Remind the children that he is one of the Evangelists; that is, he wrote one of the four Gospels. Have them look for the Gospel of St. Luke in the Bible and read a short selection about the Redeemer; for example: Luke ii. 8–20.)
24, St. Raphael, Archangel
(We shall hear more about him in the lesson on Tobias.)
28, SS. Simon and Jude, Apostles
Last Sunday in October, Feast of Christ the King.
(Long before the Redeemer came, the Prophet Isaias said of Him: "He shall sit upon the throne of David." Text, p. 211. Recall this feast when you meet the quotation in the children's text.)

The Unit Introduction:

In a few simple sentences remind the pupils again of the wonderful promise that God made to His people. Noe and his family knew of this promise and handed it down to their children. God watched with special care over these people. He knew

39

they needed good leaders, men who had great faith, and hope, and love; men who were not afraid to make sacrifices. Who some of these great leaders were and how God tried them to test their faith and trust and love, we shall learn in this unit.

Read the opening paragraph again after you have completed the unit, and let the pupils tell who the great leaders were that are referred to here.

Lessons 9 and 10

First Week in October

Aim: The aim of the lessons is to show how God guided the people He had chosen as His own and how He watched especially over, and helped, Abraham, their first great leader.

Preparation: The following words and expressions may need explaining:

Pitched their tents: Set up. They put up their tents. These people lived in tents because they moved from place to place to provide food for their cattle and sheep.

Pasture: A grassy field or hillside. Land on which grass is grown for cattle to graze.

Brethren: Brothers; sometimes also relatives, or members of the same society.

Arrive: To come to a place. Example: When did you arrive at school this morning? Mary did not arrive until nine o'clock.

Find pictures suitable for the lesson, such as pictures of Nomads living in tents.

Read Lesson 9

Take notice particularly of Abraham's kindness and thoughtfulness in letting Lot choose the best land for himself. God was pleased with his act and blessed him wonderfully. That is God's way of dealing with those who love Him. When they do just a little for love of Him, He often repays them a hundredfold even in this world; not always with riches, but often in a far better way.

Practical Application

God wants us also to be kind and thoughtful as Abraham was.

Aim to have the children acquire the "Thank you" habit. Have them practice the little scenes until they remember to say "Thank you" out of habit. However, do not let them tire doing the same thing over and over. Vary the work so that it does not become monotonous. Occasionally recall the obligation of being polite at home as well as in school.

There is much opportunity in this lesson for little dramatizations. They should, of course, be spontaneous. If the class is large, a number of small groups could play one or two little stories and have the entire class discuss what lessons each conveys. For example: A child passes a desk and accidentally knocks against a book which drops to the floor. The child excuses himself, picks up the book and returns it to the desk. The owner of the book says "Thank you." Bring the little lessons as close to the children's lives as possible.

What Would You Do if You Were in Their Place?

The discussion is intended to teach children unselfishness. Rather than bring out the fault of selfishness, make a great deal of the unselfish children mentioned and let the lesson sink in for itself.

More Things for You to Do:

4. A few of these stories, such as Healing the Blind Man, Feeding the Hungry People, Raising the Daughter of Jairus from the Dead, should be prepared ahead of time by some of the children. They could be dramatized or related to the class during another period.

5. Show that even animals prove themselves grateful. Recall the story of Androcles and the Lion.

7. If you are making this a "dramatization" week, some of the lines in the poem could be illustrated also.

For example: "Somebody did a golden deed." Pantomime: A little girl reading to a dear old grandmother.

"Somebody proved a friend in need." An old man trying to cross a busy street. A boy offers to help him across.

"Somebody sang a beautiful song." A child before a statue of the Blessed Mother or the Sacred Heart, singing a hymn.

"Somebody smiled the whole day long." Children of a family doing little errands, such as setting the table, carrying wood, caring for the baby, etc., and smiling happily as they work.

"Somebody thought, ' 'Tis sweet to live.' " Children picking flowers, feeding animals, playing, etc.

"Somebody said: 'I'm glad to give.' " A child giving food or clothing to a poor person.

Recall the good intention in connection with these little actions. It may be put something as follows: Abraham loved God. He was kind and unselfish because he knew that God would be pleased. These children also love God. They know that He is good to them and they are trying hard to do little acts of kindness to show their love for Him. Perhaps in their prayers they have told our dear Lord in words such as these: "All for Thee, dear Jesus." Jesus knows, of course, that they are doing these things for Him, but He loves to have them tell Him often, just as a mother loves to have her children come and say that they love her.

Can You Answer These Questions?

1. We can thank God for His goodness in many ways. We can often tell God how thankful we are to Him (Poem: "Father in Heaven, we Thank Thee"). We can *show* our gratitude to Him by living good lives and keeping His commandments. Through the Mass we can make a special offering of thanks to the heavenly Father, an offering far greater than that offered by Abraham, because there Jesus offers Himself for us. (Have children enumerate other ways.)

2 and 3. It is wrong to quarrel; therefore, displeases God. Quarreling is a sin against the fifth commandment.

4. To be selfish means to put ourselves and our wants ahead of others; to want the best for ourselves without considering others; to expect people to like us better than others, etc.

Words to explain for Lesson 10:

Capture: To take by force or trick. A person or animal is captured when it is caught or taken by force.

Defeat: To overcome; to gain the victory over. When someone has to give up in a contest or battle we say he has been defeated.

Teach the pronunciation of Mĕlchĭs'edĕch.

Read and Discuss Lesson 10

Dwell on two points particularly. (1) Abraham gave to Melchisedech one tenth of all he had. In the Old Testament the Jews gave one tenth of their crops, etc., for the support of the priest. Catholics also have a duty to support their priests. Discuss what children can do to help. (2) Abraham loved and served God. He would have nothing to do with the people of Sodom because they were wicked. Had he stayed with them or made friends with them, perhaps he would not have become the great leader that he was. Perhaps he would have lost his chance to become the forefather of the Redeemer.

Are You a Good Child of Your Parish?

Talk over those points which are important for your particular group. Be as specific and helpful as possible. For example, if the children are forgetful about bringing their offering on Sundays, have them think of ways of reminding themselves. Also, have them tell *how* one honors and obeys his priests and teachers: By greeting politely, by speaking well of them, by not allowing others to speak ill of them, etc.

Interesting Things for You to Do:

1. A simple activity will do; for example: drawing or cutting out vestments, or making a chart by the use of rubber stamps (see list of references, p. 172), unless the children are preparing for their First Holy Communion.

2. Make much of this. If we had no priests we would have no Mass, no Blessed Sacrament, no Confession, etc.

3. Here bring in again the obligation of making an offering to help support the Church and also of taking part in all activities that the parish offers, such as festivals, plays, etc. It must be understood, of course, that children can contribute only according to their means. Remember, however, that you are training them not only for school but for life.

4. This will be a little test of the children's knowledge on the subject.

5. This may be used as an introduction to a more detailed lesson on the Mass. Present the subject to the children as a whole first. Tell the story of the Last Supper and how Christ wished to remain with us always. Therefore He gave us the Mass. Every day at Mass He comes down on the altar to offer Himself for us and to give Himself to us. We, on our part, should go to Mass as often as possible and give ourselves to Him also. We should unite ourselves with Him in Holy Communion, just as the priest does, etc. (See references at end of lesson.)

Can You Answer These Questions?

1. The offering of Melchisedech reminds us of the Mass because Melchisedech offered bread and wine, as the priest does at Mass.

2. The first Mass was said by Jesus Himself.

3. It was said on Holy Thursday at the Last Supper.

4. The priest in the Mass changes bread and wine into the Body and Blood of Christ.

5. During Mass we should be attentive and pray the Mass with the priest. We should offer ourselves with Jesus to God the Father and, if possible, receive Him into our hearts.

6. The principal parts of the Mass are the Offertory, the Consecration, and Communion.

7. Have the children write out the name of the church or have it written on the blackboard and say a few words about the saint or mystery.

8. Make an offering regularly on Sundays, and go to parish plays, festivals, etc., show interest in all activities of the church.

9. Because the church depends entirely on the help of the people. The priest is there to help and guide them and they in turn should support him and keep up the church which is for them.

Teacher's References:

The Holy Bible, Gen. xii and xiv.

Teacher's Handbook to Bible History, "The Call of Abraham," "The Sacrifice of Melchisedech," pp. 22–26.

Biblical Questions, "The Longevity of Patriarchs," Chap. XVIII.

Catholic Action Series, Book II, Chaps. I–XII.

Teacher's Notes:

Lesson 11

Second Week in October

Aim: To show how the Lord came to visit Abraham, one of His great leaders; also to learn how we should receive Jesus when He comes to us in Holy Communion.

Preparation: Words to be explained:

Immediately: at once, right away.

Strengthened: Made stronger.

Guests: Visitors; persons who are entertained at someone else's table.

Make this an intimate lesson on Holy Communion. Teach Holy Communion as part of the Mass and not separate from it. You have already prepared the way in the foregoing lesson.

Abraham had always tried to do what God wanted of him. Now God Himself comes to visit him. What a wonderful reward for his goodness.

Read Lesson 11

Discuss the reverence Abraham showed for the Lord. Point out that God knew Sara was laughing. God sees and knows all things. He can do all things. It is the same today as it was then.

Why was Abraham so eager to have a son? Because he, too, was waiting for the Redeemer and hoping that he would come from his family.

Let the children tell what Abraham did for his visitors and what they would do for the Lord if He really came to see them.

It is taken for granted that children of this grade have already received their First Holy Communion. This is simply a reminder of the things they have already been taught. Should it happen that the children have not yet received their First Holy Communion, this lesson may be taken more in detail and reviewed later when the immediate preparation begins. In that case use the lesson more to excite a real longing for Jesus in the Blessed Sacrament.

Take as much time as you need for this lesson, especially if you feel that a thorough review is necessary. Have the children *do* certain acts, such as showing how to go to the altar rail, how to open their mouths, etc.

Do not forget that Holy Communion is an intimate part of the Mass. The Mass is a sacrifice in which we all have part. We should not be mere spectators but participants.

Poems and hymns in honor of the Blessed Sacrament should be used at the psychological moment; that is, just at the moment when they fit in best. In case the children are preparing for First Holy Communion they could start "My Communion Booklet" at this time and work on it occasionally as their preparation proceeds.

Now Can You Answer These Questions?

1. Holy Communion is the receiving of the Body and Blood of Jesus Christ.

2. To make a good Communion it is necessary to be without mortal sin, and to fast from midnight on.

3. Anyone in danger of death is allowed to receive Holy Communion without fasting.

4. We must receive Holy Communion at least once a year at Easter time.

5. We may and should receive Holy Communion every day, if possible.

Other questions may be added here, depending upon the preparation the class has had.

Teacher's References:

The Holy Bible, Gen. xviii.

Teacher's Handbook to Bible History, "Abraham's Faith and Hospitality," pp. 22–27.

Catholic Action Series, Book II, "The Communion," pp. 70, 71.

Teacher's Notes:

Lessons 12 and 13

Third Week in October

Aim: The two lessons show again, in a striking manner, God's hatred of sin on the one hand, and on the other, His readiness to reward those who love and serve Him. God's holiness, His justice, His mercy, and His providence are well illustrated in the stories of the Old Testament. Aim to make the children more fully aware of these attributes of God as they read the lessons of Sodom and Gomorrah and Abraham's obedience. Strive to impress them on the minds of the pupils so that they will recall them not only for the time being but in particular in later life. For that purpose it may be well to associate the lessons with the joys and sorrows of everyday life and to show pupils that God still cares for us in the same way as He did for His Chosen People.

Preparation: Words to be explained:

The Just: Those that live an upright life.

Spare: To show mercy; to save; to keep from harm or punishment. Abraham was a *just* man; that is, he was a good, upright man, who tried to do the will of God. He asked God to *spare* the people of the wicked cities; that is, not to punish them.

If possible show pictures referring to the lesson.

Read Lesson 12

Bring out the attributes of God as shown in the lesson.

God knew the wickedness of the people. He knows and sees all things. God showed His willingness to spare them for the sake of a few good people. He is merciful. God destroyed the cities by sending fire from heaven. He is all powerful. He can do all things. God hates and punishes sin. He is holy and just. God watched over Abraham and his family. He cares for those who serve and love Him. Once before, God had shown His great hatred of sin by destroying many people. When (Deluge)?

Practical Application

Ask questions regarding sin in order to discover whether the pupils have the necessary knowledge. For the time being do not go into detail any more than necessary. Speak more at length on the wickedness of mortal sin and aim at arousing sorrow for sin. Let the children tell in their own words what they should say to God to show that they are sorry for their sins. Stress God's love for them.

When, by means of the lesson, you have impressed upon the

pupils God's hatred of sin, review the act of contrition which the children ordinarily use. Ask such questions as the following: Which sentence tells that you are sorry because you have offended God? Which tells that you are sorry because you deserve to be punished? If you were telling your mother how sorry you are for doing something wrong, which do you think would please her most: to say that you are sorry because she is so good to you and you have hurt her, or that you are sorry because she is going to punish you?

When we are sorry for our sins because we have offended the good God, we have *perfect* contrition. When we are sorry because we have lost heaven and deserved hell, we have *imperfect* contrition. Which of the two is better? In which sentence do you tell God that you will do better?

Words to explain for Lesson 13:

Only begotten son: Simply mention that Isaac was the only son that Sarah and Abraham had.

Worship: To show respect and honor to God.

Victim: The animal or person to be sacrificed.

Ram: A sheep.

Type: We speak of persons in the Old Testament as being types of Christ, etc., because they are in some ways like Him and were intended by God to represent Him.

Before reading Lesson 13 have the children tell what great promises God made to Abraham. Look back at Lesson 9 to find them. Abraham trusted God. He knew God would keep His word.

Now Read and Discuss Lesson 13

Notice how promptly Abraham obeyed. He could not understand how God could ask such a thing, but he trusted Him just the same.

The activity following the lesson is intended to show the children how the Chosen People always kept in mind the wonderful promise made in Paradise and how it was handed down from father to son. From time to time go back to the first promise in Paradise and then trace it through the different epochs so as to unify the entire Old Testament and show its purpose as the foreshadowing of the Redeemer.

Can You Answer These Questions?

1 and 2. We should make an act of contrition before going to bed at night, after having committed a mortal sin, and before confession.

3. No, because Isaac was only a man and Jesus was man and God. The difference between sacrificing a man and God's sacrifice of Himself is so great that we cannot fully understand it.

4. Jesus Christ is the Son of God, the second person of the Blessed Trinity.

5. There are three persons in God: The Father, the Son, and the Holy Ghost. (Other questions may be added here for review, if desired.)

6. God promised a Redeemer because when Adam and Eve sinned in Paradise, heaven was closed for them and all who would come after them. God felt sorry for us and sent His Son, Jesus, to "make up" for the sin of our first parents and to open heaven again.

Teacher's References:

The Holy Bible, Gen. xix and xxii.

Teacher's Handbook to Bible History, "The Destruction of Sodom and Gomorrah," "The Sacrifice of Isaac," pp. 28–31.

Biblical Questions, "Sodom and Gomorrha," pp. 123–125.

Catholic Action Series, Book I, "Contrition," pp. 159–162.

Teacher's Notes:

Lessons 14, 15, and 16

Fourth Week in October

Aim: To show in the stories of Isaac and his two sons, how God lets all things happen for our own good. Rebecca met Eliezer as if by accident, but in reality she came in answer to his prayer. Jacob received the blessing of his father by an act of injustice, but he had really been destined by God to become the leader of his people.

Preparation: Words to explain:

Spring: A fountain of water.

To draw water means to pull up water or dip water from a spring.

Store here means plenty.

Meantime: In the time between or in the time that followed.

Favorite: Best loved.

Pottage: A kind of soup.

Kid: The young of a goat.

Mock: To make fun of someone.

Fetch: To go and bring.

Garments: Clothes.

Dew: The water which stands in small drops on plants, etc., after a cool night.

Fatness of the earth: Fruitfulness or richness of the earth.

Tribe: A large group or family of people belonging together.

Read for yourself the explanation of Jacob's act in Bandas, *Biblical Questions,* pp. 126–129.

As a secondary activity, have the children find as many pictures as possible showing people at prayer. Be careful, however, to keep well in mind the example taken from the lesson itself.

Appoint the groups for the plays and pantomimes ahead of time and let them make their own plans. Be sure to include the Biblical Stories themselves in the dramatization.

Read and Discuss Lesson 14

Where was Abraham's own country? Have the pupils look back to Lesson 9 to find out.

Call attention to the willingness of Rebecca to serve others. Notice also that Eliezer did not forget to thank the Lord for hearing his prayer.

Bring out the power of prayer. Give as much attention to the subject as you can. Strive to make prayer more intelligible and more natural for the children.

Giving a Play: It is well to show the children just *how* certain actions are done. Dramatization or pantomime will be a great aid in this lesson. Form the groups and have the children go through all the actions and prayers that fit in. If you need any suggestions see *Practical Aids,* by Sister Aurelia and Father Kirsch; also *Catholic School Journal,* March, 1934; "The Play Comes to the Aid of the Teacher." Help the children to a better understanding of the prayers they usually say as a matter of routine. Point out that when we pray we talk to God. We should often talk to God in our own way. Ask the children to tell what they would say, for example, before beginning to study. Just a simple, "Dear God, please help me to study my lessons," is sufficient. Occasionally stop to make a little prayer for them. For example, after a dreary season, the sun comes out beautifully. "Dear God," the teacher might have them say, "thank you for the lovely sunshine that brightens up the world," etc.

Let the children sing often, choosing such songs as fit into the lesson. Here, for example, "Jesus, Teach Me How to Pray," would be timely.

Explain the Scripture text.

Can You Answer These Questions?

Review the more important prayers to make sure that the children say them correctly.

1. Prayer is speaking to God. (Show how Eliezer spoke to God.)

2. We should pray every morning and evening, before and after meals, on Sundays and holydays, in all dangers, in temptation, in sorrow, etc.

3. We should pray with attention, that is, know what we are talking about and to whom we are talking. When we pray we should remember that God can do all things and that we of our own accord can do nothing. We should trust in God's goodness to give us what we ask, and continue to pray if we are not heard at once. (How many of these qualities of prayer can be found in the lesson?)

4. God always answers our prayers, but not always in the way in which we expect. A prayer is never lost. God knows what is best for us.

Other questions that may be asked about prayer:

What prayers do you know?

Which prayer did our Lord Himself teach us?

Is it wrong to be distracted during prayer? (Explain that there is no wrong unless we *want* the distraction. Try to form the habit, however, of being as attentive as possible, while talking to God.)

An appropriate text that may be added, is: "Ask and it shall be given to you." (Matt. vii. 2.)

Read Lessons 15 and 16

Be sure that the children understand fully the introductory remark, as it deals with the theme, so to speak, of the Old Testament; namely, the Promise of the Redeemer and how much it meant to God's Chosen People.

Let the children give examples of selling their birthright, such as, staying in bed Sunday mornings instead of attending Mass, eating meat on Fridays, etc.

Practical Application

Discuss mortal sin, which is the selling of our spiritual birthright. Illustrate each of the three points by specific examples, such as the following:

1. John tells his mother that he lost two cents of the change the grocer gave him. John has the money in his pocket. He knows he is telling a lie. He has made up his mind ahead of time that he is going to tell his mother he lost the money. Has he committed a mortal sin? Which of the three requirements is wanting?

2. Ellen comes home very hungry one afternoon. She goes to the frigidaire and gets a piece of ham which she eats with great relish. Afterwards she remembers that it is Friday.

3. A neighborhood gang call Johnny, who is not one of their number, to go into a store with them and, while they are talking to the clerk, to steal a valuable ring. They tell him they will kill him if he does not do as they say. Johnny does not want to steal, but he is very much frightened. They take him along and he steals the ring for them.

Have the class recall how terribly God punished sin: The bad angels, Adam and Eve, The Deluge, Sodom and Gomorrah.

Can You Answer These Questions?

1. Mortal sin is a great offense against the law of God.
2. Answer according to text, page 59.
3. Mortal sin can be forgiven by a good confession.
4. Yes, mortal sin can also be forgiven by an act of perfect

contrition, with the intention of going to confession.

5. Christ gave the power to forgive sins to His Apostles when He said: "Receive ye the Holy Ghost. Whose sins you shall forgive, they are forgiven them; whose sins you shall retain, they are retained."

Explain, if necessary, why a sin is called "mortal." It brings supernatural *death* to the soul.

Teacher's References:

The Holy Bible, Gen. xxiv, xxv, and xxvii.

Teacher's Handbook to Bible History, "Isaac Married Rebecca," "Esau and Jacob," pp. 31–35.

Biblical Questions, "Esau and Jacob," pp. 126–129.

Catholic Action Series, "Sin," pp. 143–148; "Prayer," pp. 291–296.

Teacher's Notes:

Lessons 17 and 18

First Week in November

Aim: To learn how, in Jacob's dream of God, the future leader received once more the promise of a Redeemer.

Preparation: Have pictures of beautiful churches posted on the bulletin board. Under the pictures might appear the words: "This is no other but the house of God and the gate of heaven!" Explain the following words if necessary:

Trembling: Shaking as with fear.

Custom: The way it has always been; the way people generally do things.

Deceive: To make others believe something that is not true.

In my service: To work for me.

Labors: All his work.

Discovered: Found out.

Jealous: Full of envy. Afraid that someone else might get ahead or be liked better.

Secretly: On the sly, without letting anyone know.

Shearing: Cutting off the wool from the sheep.

Before reading the story have the children review the lesson which shows the relationship of Jacob's mother with Laban (Lesson 14).

Read Lesson 17

Jacob, having received the blessing of the firstborn, was to take the place of the eldest son, and act as priest; that is, offer the sacrifice for the family or tribe.

Interesting Things to Do:

1. Plan this work according to the needs of the class. It can be made very helpful in calling attention to little faults, because it comes from the pupils in the form of a pleasant activity rather than as a rebuke. Dramatize the little actions, such as entering the church, making the genuflection, etc., if desired. Recall, at times, Jacob's words: "This is no other but the house of God and the gate of heaven."

2. If there is any abuse as to care of the pews, etc., this

would offer an opportunity to impress upon the pupils the respect we owe to things belonging to the house of God. A word about raising flowers for the use of the altar later in their lives, may prove an inspiration to someone.

The Good Things to Read offer helpful material.

Can You Answer These Questions?

1. Jesus Christ founded the Catholic Church.

2. The pope, the successor of St. Peter, is the visible head of the Church.

3. The pope lives in Rome in a palace called the Vatican.

4. The present pope (1935) is Pius XI.

5. Catholics make a genuflection in church because they know that Jesus is present in the Blessed Sacrament.

6. Jesus comes down on the altar at the consecration of the Mass.

7. Jesus comes down on the altar for us, that He may offer Himself to God for us and give Himself to us during the Holy Communion of the Mass.

8. We should show that we understand that Jesus is present on the altar.

Read Lesson 18

If there is any question, explain simply that in the Old Testament God allowed the Patriarchs to have more than one wife.

Recall that Jacob was to stay but a short time, according to the plans of Rebecca. It was twenty years, however, before he could return to his own home.

Teacher's References:

The Holy Bible, Gen. xxviii and xxix.

Teacher's Handbook to Bible History, "Jacob Journeys to Laban," pp. 35–36.

Catholic Action Series, Book I, "Thoughts for Us," pp. 9–10.

Teacher's Notes:

Lesson 19

Second Week in November

Aim: As the title suggests, the lesson aims to impress upon us Esau's forgiveness, which enabled Jacob to return home to his own family. It also shows Jacob's willingness to share what he had with his brother.

Preparation: Read over the problems and Interesting Things to Do and make your plans accordingly. Find as many pictures as possible to help bring home the lessons involved. There are many stories written to show how noble people, especially the saints, forgave their enemies. The example of Christ upon the cross should be supreme, of course. The words "He forgave His enemies" or similar ones may be added to a picture of the crucifixion.

Words to be explained:

Deliver me: Save me.

Offend: To hurt one's feelings.

Wrestle: To try to throw one another down.

Accepted: Took what was offered.

In the last lesson we saw Jacob on his way home. What might he have been afraid of? We shall see how his brother received him.

Read Lesson 19

Notice especially the words "Take of the blessings which I have brought you and which God, who gives all things, has given me." Jacob realized that his riches and all he had came from God.

What Would You Do in Their Place?

Point out that we, too, must be willing to forgive others.

Two lessons are brought out in the problems: Forgiveness and willingness to share with others. Let the children give their own reactions. Be careful not to let them get into the habit of anticipating what the teacher expects them to answer. Try to convince them of the right rather than merely to let them guess what is expected of them. "What would Jesus have done in such a case?" might help to answer the question.

It may be pointed out, too, that one may feel hurt or angry but that it is the intention to do the right thing that counts. For example: In Problem 4, Mildred could not help but feel disappointed, especially if she had made plans of her own. However, in spite of her feelings, she could have told her mother that she was willing to stay at home; and she should have treated her sister kindly.

1. Have two boys or two girls show in word and action what they would do.

2. Of course, Marie would feel badly about her doll. But since it was an accident she should treat Dorine kindly.

3. Discuss: "Never let the sun go down on your anger."

4. Show how Mildred, if she were a splendid little girl, would act.

5. Discuss and have the children give reasons for their answers.

6. In this and the following problems the discussion should bring out the way a well-trained and unselfish child should act. It should at least suggest unselfish actions so that they come to mind when the occasion presents itself.

7. Some children will be found to save candy that they receive in school so that they might share it with mother when they get home. It is in this way that children are trained to be thoughtful of others.

8. If Violet were told to spend all her money, she might make a lovely little feast by having all the members of the family share in the celebration. Have the children suggest little plans of their own. If Violet were a very poor little girl, it might be well to get something useful or to save at least part of the money. At any rate, pleasure and profit might be combined for herself in the way she uses the money.

9. Another suggestion of thoughtfulness for others without too much sacrifice on the part of the owner.

10. Answers will vary according to circumstances. She might share the pleasure with her family by brightening up the home with the flowers, she might give some to a person who seldom has such a pleasure, to someone who is sick, or perhaps for use on the altar in church.

Interesting Things for You to Do:

2. Feast of St. Gualbert, July 12.

3. Any little scene or series of scenes appealing to the children may be used.

4. For a better understanding of the various prayers and peti-

tions contained in the Our Father, teach some of the little poems contained in *The Our Father for Little Ones* (The Catechetical Guild, St. Paul, Minn.)

5. If there is time, let the children find such poems and stories in different readers. Do not forget to recall the story of Esau and Jacob in connection with the work.

Can You Answer These Questions?

1. When we have offended other people we should ask them to forgive us. We should do this especially when we have offended our parents or others in whose charge we are placed.

2. We should ask God to forgive us.

3. God is willing to forgive us as often as we are truly sorry for our sins and ask His forgiveness.

4. The priest gives us a penance after confession that we may make up to God for the temporal punishment that we have merited for our sins. (If necessary, discuss here the two kinds of punishment due to sin, namely *temporal* and *eternal* punishment, and the chief means by which we satisfy God for the temporal punishment: prayer, fasting, almsgiving, all spiritual and corporal works of mercy, and patience in sufferings of all kinds.)

5. People who die with sins on their souls cannot go to heaven.

6. They go to purgatory if they have only venial sins on their souls and to hell if they have even one mortal sin on their souls.

Teacher's References:

The Holy Bible, Gen. xxxiii.

Teacher's Handbook to Bible History, "Jacob's Return Home," pp. 36–37.

Catholic Action Series, Book I, "Forgiveness," pp. 166–168.

Teacher's Notes:

Lesson 20

Third Week in November

Aim: To hear the story of Joseph and to learn from it how God permitted evil to happen to him in order that great good might come to the Children of Israel. Also, to learn a prompt and cheerful obedience to parents.

Preparation: Explain such words as the following:

Strange dream: A dream that was different, that made him wonder.

Binding: Tying into bundles.

Sheaf: A bundle of grain.

Subjects: Those who are under the power of another. All who belong to and owe obedience to a person, especially to a king.

Devour: To eat.

Shed: To pour out.

Merchant: One who buys and sells.

Pit: A deep hole.

He would not be comforted: That is, no matter what his sons did to make him forget his sorrow, he could not be cheered.

Cheerfully: Gladly.

Promptly: At once, quickly.

If the children could see some of Tissot's pictures in colors, they would understand better what a coat of many colors might have looked like. The Tissot pictures, although they lack a great deal of the supernatural and reverent, are most suggestive as far as oriental coloring and background are concerned. (See list of references.)

The stories pertaining to Joseph are among the most interesting in the Old Testament. Be sure that the children get all they can out of them. Get the connection between one and the other by means of review questions that help to establish the relationship of the stories.

Read Lesson 20

Talk about Joseph's answer "I am ready." What does it show? Over and above everything else, keep in mind God's watchful care over the nation that was destined to bring forth the Redeemer.

Practical Application

Discuss the sentences referring to obedience. In this lesson stress principally obedience to parents.

Show that parents also have a duty toward their children; that sometimes they must punish their children even though it hurts them more than the children; that God will punish parents and teachers if they do not do their duty in bringing up the children for Him.

Dwell on each of the quotations and explain whatever is not clear, by simple examples. Little dramatizations could again serve to illustrate, while the class recite the quotations together.

"Robin's Disobedience" could be illustrated by a series of posters and also made into a little play.

Do not lose sight of the main interest, the story of Joseph itself. Come back to it occasionally in your discussions.

More Things for You to Do:

Since the lesson on obedience is so important, try to use various means to impress it upon the minds of the pupils. The stories read by the children might also be dramatized. Make much particularly of Christ's obedience to His parents, although He was God and therefore much greater than they.

Can You Answer These Questions?

1. The dreams that Joseph and other holy men had, were not the same as our dreams. They were really more like pictures of messages sent by God to tell these men something about themselves or the future.

2. The dreams we have do not ordinarily come from God and they therefore mean nothing special.

3. We should not believe in dreams or fortune-tellers. It is a sin to do so.

4. We must obey our parents because we were given to them by God who gave them a right over us and expects us to do as they say as long as it is not sinful.

5. We must also obey our teachers and other superiors.

6 and 7. Yes, parents must take care of their children, teach them how to live properly, and especially how to know and love and serve God so that they may live with Him in heaven after they die.

Teacher's References:
  The Holy Bible, Gen. xxxvii.
  Teacher's Handbook to Bible History, "Joseph's Dream,"
pp. 38–39.
  Catholic Action Series, Book II, "Obedience is the Founda-
tion of the Home," pp. 290–295.
Teacher's Notes:

Lesson 21

Fourth Week in November

Aim: To learn with Joseph, to keep away from sin, especially the sin of impurity, and to understand, also, that as the Lord protected Joseph, He will protect all those who trust in Him.

Preparation: While we learn in this lesson more about the fate of Joseph, we can also make use of the story as a special preparation for the coming feast of the Immaculate Conception. Naturally we should stress the beauty of purity more than the ugliness of the sin of impurity. Look over the activities and decide on those that will be most interesting and helpful to the class.

Words to explain:

Entire: Whole.

Tempt: To try to make someone do what he does not wish to or may not do. (Show the difference between tempting to do what one merely does not wish to do and what is forbidden and sinful, by practical illustrations.)

Cherish: To hold dear.

Trust in God: The belief that God will help those who put their hope in Him.

Valor: Bravery.

Upheld: Kept from falling; kept free from danger and harm.

Read Lesson 21

The story shows how Joseph's goodness was recognized by both Putiphar and the keeper of the prison. Which quotation at the end of the lesson gives us a reason?

Dwell on the words, "The Lord was with him, as He had always been." Show that God is with those that love and serve Him, no matter what happens.

Practical Application

The sentences following the lesson will require explanation and discussion. It is important, just at this age, that the children get correct notions of right and wrong. Encourage the children to choose the sentences that best help them in their own lives. But, be simple and practical. For example, "I must be clean in thought" may not at first be clear to the children. Show how important it is that we control not only our actions but also our thoughts. Refer again to the lesson on Cain and Abel. Cain entertained wicked thoughts first, then he carried them out in action. Joseph must have kept away from his mind all evil thoughts, or he could not have resisted the temptation. Our actions are usually the result of our thoughts. Because our thoughts are not seen, they cannot be checked by others. We must be all the more careful ourselves to check them and keep them always pure and good. Teach the children by direct example how they can check evil thoughts. They should know that sin does not enter in until we take pleasure in a thought and actually want to keep it in mind.

"Bad language" may mean something altogether different to one child than to another. Try to point out the difference between vulgar and improper language, on the one hand, and immoral and sinful language, on the other.

The teacher must be very cautious not to make sin where there is none and thus create a false conscience in the child. Stress the good and beautiful wherever possible.

"An idle brain is the devil's workshop" will need explanation. When a child sits around doing nothing, we may be sure the devil will get busy suggesting evil thoughts. Children who are always busy doing something worth while, like reading, sewing, building houses, playing ball, etc., do not find time to think evil thoughts. It is the children who are too quiet, who are sitting still and doing nothing, who are usually tempted to think and do evil.

Joseph knew that God knows and sees everything. That thought should be the guiding principle in this respect. It is a lesson which the child must carry through life, if he is to live in accordance with God's law. All other motives break down under great stress. The thought of God and of His rewards and punishments alone is lasting.

If the lesson is used in preparation for the Feast of the Immaculate Conception, a booklet might be made in honor of the Blessed Mother this week. "Mary, Mother of Purity" or "Mary our Model" might be the title.

More Things for You to Do:

1. It cannot be remarked too often that the problems are a great aid in developing thought and right attitudes, provided the teacher uses them properly.

2. Let the children choose the quotation they like best.

3. The lily, if large enough, may be used for a booklet. A copy can be hectographed for each child.

4. Have the children tell what they like about the life of one or the other of the saints, if there is time.

5. It is important that a Catholic calendar be kept in the classroom, or better still, that there be one in each home. Since Christmas is drawing near, it might be suggested that a good calendar be given as a gift to the family.

7. This might be made a little language exercise. Use the quotation occasionally at a patriotic or other program. (In fact, the selections and dramatizations, etc., developed in this book, should often be reviewed, not mechanically, but in an impromptu program or in connection with another lesson. In this way the work is reviewed without resorting to mechanical drill.)

Can You Answer These Questions?

1. I can keep my heart pure by prayer, by keeping away from bad company, by receiving the sacraments often, etc.

2. Yes, children can sin with their eyes by looking at evil things, reading bad books, looking at bad pictures, etc.

3. Children can sin with their ears by listening with pleasure to evil talk. They can sin in their thoughts by thinking and wanting evil thoughts.

4. If someone tempts me to sin I should pray for help (What prayer?), go away from the person if possible, think how God hates and punishes sin, and how good He has been to me.

5. Yes, God knows everything that I think.

6. God is all-knowing. He sees and knows everything, even our most secret thoughts.

Teacher's References:

The Holy Bible, Gen. xxxvii.

Teacher's Handbook to Bible History, "Joseph Sold by His Brethren," pp. 30–40; "Joseph in the House of Putiphar," pp. 40–42.

Catholic Action Series, Book II, "Holy Purity," pp. 334–347, especially 346.

Teacher's Notes:

Lessons 22 and 23

Fifth Week in November

Aim: In these two lessons we note again that God's Providence watches over us and turns all things to our good. The whole history of the Old Testament, in fact, is a striking and clear proof of God's Providence, showing that He orders all things for our own good. Aim to impress this thought more deeply upon the children.

Preparation: As an approach to the story, read and discuss the poem "The Tempest" by James T. Fields, or any other poem or story emphasizing God's Providence. In the course of the discussion lead to God's care of Joseph, the Forgotten Prisoner.

The following words may need explanation:

Butler: The chief servant in a house.

Banquet: A feast in which excellent food is served.

Lean: Thin.

Ears: The full fruit of a stalk of grain or corn.

Stalk: The stem.

Plenty: All that one needs.

Famine: A want of food; a time of starving.

Explanation: A telling of the meaning of something.

Advice: Directions or opinion of what should be done.

Robe: Garment.

Chariot: A two-wheeled wagon drawn by horses.

Announced: Called out, told.

Fruitful years: The years in which there was plenty of grain.

The two lessons offer splendid suggestions for activities of all kinds, including drawing, poster work, and dramatization.

Read Lesson 22

Answer the questions and talk about the picture.

The butler forgot about Joseph when all went well with him again. Do you think Joseph forgot to thank God when he was protected especially by Him?

In order to bring this little lesson more closely into their own lives, dramatize a scene such as the following: Mary has been praying that a very sick little brother may get well again. One day when she comes home from school, little brother is better and the doctor has said that he is out of danger. Instinctively, Mary folds her hands and says: "Oh, thank You, dear Lord, You have made us so happy. You are so good, to hear our prayers." (Or, in a more formal way, the mother may gather her children around her, tell them the good news, and then and there have them kneel down and say a prayer of thanks.)

Read Lesson 23

Two years passed, and Joseph was still in prison. How must he have felt? Did he murmur against God? We can see now that God had a big surprise for Joseph, but Joseph did not know about that. Just the same, he trusted God. He did not feel as though God had forgotten all about him.

By practical examples from real life show how we sometimes misunderstand God's goodness. God sends a man sickness. During the time of good health the man thought little about God and his own soul. During his sickness he makes his peace with God, learns how to pray again, and is reminded that sooner or later he will have to die and his soul return to God. What this man thought to be an evil was really a blessing in disguise.

Interesting Things for You to Do:

Use this opportunity to cultivate devotion to St. Joseph. Make sure, however, that the children distinguish between Joseph of Egypt and St. Joseph, the foster father of the Redeemer. The Church now uses the words of Pharao, "Go to Joseph," to remind us that St. Joseph, too, can help us, just as Joseph of Egypt helped the poor, starving people that came to him. While speaking of Egypt, you might point out that it was to this country that Joseph and Mary had to take the child Jesus shortly after His birth, to save Him from death.

"The Man of the House" should be read and perhaps memorized by the children. (See Good Things to Read.)

Can You Answer These Questions?

1. St. Joseph is the foster father of Jesus and the legal husband of Mary, the Mother of God.

2. St. Joseph is in heaven now.

3. Heaven is the place where we see God face to face and are happy with Him forever.

4. Not all go directly to heaven.

5. They who die with mortal sin on their souls go to hell.

6. They who die with venial sins, go to purgatory.

Teacher's References:

The Holy Bible, Gen. xl, xli.

Teacher's Handbook to Bible History, "Joseph in Prison," "Joseph's Elevation," pp. 42–46.

Catholic Action Series, Book II, "God's Care for Those Who Live by the Law of Love," pp. 424–426.

Teacher's Notes:

Lessons 24 and 25

First Week in December

Aim: To hear further the story of Joseph and his brothers during the famine and thereby to learn to take better care of our own food, clothing, etc.

Preparation: Explain the following words:

Scarce: Not plentiful, not enough.

Interpreter: A person whose business it is to translate words spoken in a foreign language. In this story, a person who was able to understand the language of Joseph's brothers and also the Egyptian language. He had to tell Joseph what the brothers were saying and the brothers what Joseph was saying.

Astonished: Surprised.

Troubled: Worried; wondering what was going to happen; disturbed.

Approach the lesson by talking about the causes of famine. Depression is a word better known to the children. Famine pertains more to food, of course, but in the long run the results are very much the same.

We know there was a famine in Egypt. Now it spread also to Chanaan, the home of Joseph's father and brothers. They needed food badly. Let us see what they did to get it.

Read Lesson 24

Discuss the lesson thoroughly after the first reading.

"He thought of the dream he had when he was a boy." What was the dream he thought of? Look for Lesson 20.

"We deserve to suffer these things" — What did this admission prove to Joseph?

Read Lesson 25

Why was Jacob so unwilling to let Benjamin go to Egypt? Why do you think Joseph wanted him?

Why were the brothers surprised to find that they were seated according to their age?

Practical Application

Explain that wastefulness is always wrong, even on the part of those who can afford to be wasteful. Food and clothing are God's gifts. They must not be misused. Show also that waste of time may be as great or greater a fault than waste of food, etc.

This lesson offers opportunity for much profitable discussion. Have the pupils watch themselves during school hours to see whether they waste time in getting out their books, preparing for an exercise, etc. Help them form desirable habits in getting ready promptly for their lessons and activities.

Discuss each of the sentences following the lesson and illustrate with practical examples.

After realizing that all comes from the hands of God, the children should be better able to say the prayers before and after meals with a fuller understanding of their meaning. Review these prayers and explain them again, if necessary.

Using Good Judgment:

1. Of course all the children will know what should be done in this case. Carry out the lesson in dialog form, showing what might be said in each of the three cases. Point out also the effect on mother and father. Mother feels sad, as it is, even if she does not show it to the children. Edna's conduct will either help them bear the burden more easily or make life all the harder for them.

2. Food should never be wasted. It is a gift of God. Someone else may be glad for it. Food that cannot be used for people is usually fed to the animals so that it is not wasted.

3. Jim is not right. His father would not approve of his throwing away money; and that is what Jim is actually doing.

4. Inez did not use good judgment. She could have invested her money better in many ways. For example, she might have saved some of it, bought a good book, bought something useful, etc. Let the children add examples. The aim is to make them aware of the fact that a wise choice brings better results in the long run. Take the examples given, for instance, and show

in each case, whether the money spent would still be doing service in a week, a month, a year?

5. If Fred was a poor boy and the cap would have to be supplied by another, Fred did not use good judgment. Much would depend on the circumstances here. If, for example, the cap was a cheap advertisement that he picked up somewhere and that his mother did not care to have him wear, he might have used good judgment by not keeping the boys waiting. Usually, of course, the former is the case.

6. It is not always kindness to give away what we have. Dan must learn to say "No."

7. Discuss what Annie might do with the food. Don't forget the birds.

8. He is not showing good judgment, first of all because it is not at all funny to mark up other people's houses and break down their fences. He has the wrong idea about fun. Then, too, he has no right over other people's property. He is responsible for any damage he may do. Speak here also of the pride we should have in the appearance of our homes, yards, books, etc.

9. Since the property does not belong to the boys, they have no right to destroy it, even if they think it will not be used. It is not so much a question of whether the property is to be used again or not, as it is that the boys themselves do what is right and omit doing what is wrong.

10. The flowers in the park are kept there for the enjoyment of everyone passing by. The keepers are paid for caring for them and the people pay taxes for the upkeep of the parks. Impress upon the children their responsibility for public property. In the long run the destruction of public property falls back on the people themselves because either they can no longer enjoy the property or they must pay to have it replaced.

The sayings will require explanation.

The Famine from "Hiawatha" will correlate well with these lessons.

"The Lost Hour" is well worth memorizing. (See Good Things to Read.)

Can You Answer These Questions?

1. We may not damage other people's property because it does not belong to us and we have no right over it.

2. We may not take what does not belong to us. That is stealing.

3. We may not keep what we find if it has any value. We must try to find the owner.

4. Food and clothing are gifts of God. What God gives us may not be wasted, because He gave it to us for use.

5. God gives us the things we need for life. He gives us our parents and they must provide us with the gifts which God gives to the world.

6. We can show ourselves grateful by being careful not to waste God's gifts, by thanking Him often for them, and by sharing with others when they are in need. The Christmas season, which is close at hand, is an excellent time for teaching lessons of generosity and also of gratitude for God's gifts. God gave us His only Son, Jesus, on Christmas Day, that He might become our Little Brother and our Redeemer. Tie up the lesson with the season.

Teacher's References:

The Holy Bible, Gen. xlii, xliii.

The Teacher's Handbook to Bible History, "The Famine in Egypt," "Second Journey to Egypt," pp. 46–50.

Teacher's Notes:

Lessons 26, 27, and 28

Second Week in December

Aim: The lessons aim to show Joseph's willingness to repay good for evil and the love he bore for his father.

Preparation: Plan the work of these three lessons, especially the character traits to be brought out, according to the needs of your own class.

Words to explain:

Hard-hearted: Without feeling for others.

Steward: The manager of the house.

Overtake: To follow after and catch up with.

Plead: To beg.

Linger: To stay a while longer.

Embrace: To take into one's arms.

Robe: Garment; a beautiful gown.

Ill-treated: To treat badly or harshly.

Quarrelsome: Quarreling easily; fond of fighting.

Before reading the lesson, recall the important facts of the last story.

Read Lesson 26

Ask such questions as the following: Why had the brothers been jealous of Joseph? Why was the cup put into Benjamin's sack? Had the brothers reason to be jealous of Benjamin? (The father really showed a preference for him as he had shown for Joseph.) Do you think that the brothers had become better men? How do you know?

Read Lesson 27

How could Joseph say that it was God who sent him to Egypt? Talk about Joseph's noble forgiveness of his brothers after they had treated him so shamefully that they had even wanted to kill him. Notice his great love for his father. In your dramatizations of these lessons use the Biblical words when possible. They are so beautiful. For example: "Go now quickly to my father," etc.

Do You Show Good Sportsmanship?

Let the children give other examples. Refer to these remarks when you notice behavior such as is mentioned here. Preferably, commend the children for their good sportsmanship. You might say: "Today I saw . . ." without mentioning any particular name. In this way a number of children who may have tried hard to show good sportsmanship will feel that their efforts are being noticed. The practical application and reminder should come frequently from the children themselves. "Sister, that was showing good sportsmanship" a child might say after a contest, when the losing captain and his group cheer the winners. Be on the alert for classroom situations at all times, to help you put over the lessons in their natural setting.

Read Lesson 28

Notice especially Jacob's touching words. Have the children use them in their dramatization. "Fear not, go down to Egypt . . ." Jacob, we know, had received his father's special blessing, which brought with it the Promise of the Redeemer. Here Jacob receives God's assurance that he is doing the right thing by leaving Chanaan, the Promised Land. See how much these great leaders depended on the guidance of God.

Notice the generosity of Pharao. He gives Jacob and his sons a choice of the best lands.

Teacher's References:

The Holy Bible, Gen. xlv, xlvii.

Teacher's Handbook to Bible History, "Jacob Journeying to Egypt," pp. 53–55.

Catholic Action Series, "Spiritual Works of Mercy," pp. 273–275.

Teacher's Notes:

Lessons 29 and 30

Third Week in December

Aim: Lesson 29 completes the stories of Joseph and points more clearly to the coming of the Redeemer. Lesson 30 aims to teach, from the story of Job, that we, too, can show patience in a hundred different ways all our own, and learn to conform our wills to the will of God, just as this holy man did.

Preparation: Words to explain:

Expectation: The person expected.

Mourn: To show sorrow at the loss of a person.

The entire story of Joseph lends itself to dramatizations in a special way. In fact, there are a number of plays now written. See *Wonder Stories of God's People,* page 51, and *Catholic School Journal,* March, 1931.

In a few sentences recall how Jacob came to live in Egypt.

Read Lesson 29

The quotation "The scepter shall not be taken away from Juda, till He comes that is to be sent, and He shall be the expectation of nations" is of the greatest importance, as it draws together past and future lessons. Have the children memorize it after they understand its meaning. Show a picture of a scepter, which is a sign of power (see picture, page 225).

So far we have known only that the Messiah is to come from the Chosen People. Now we hear something more. From now on we shall remember that as long as Juda shall not be ruled by another nation, the Messiah is not to be expected.

Practical Application

Love and thoughtfulness for parents may well be tied up with the happy little surprises of the Christmas season. Let the children tell what they can do and omit doing to make Christmas a very happy time for all at home. Perhaps the little Advent practices could center around these little activities so that love for the Christ Child may be made the motive power.

The poem "Which Loved Best" can be found in a number of readers. See *Practical Aids.*

Can You Answer These Questions?

1. God tells us to love and obey our parents.

2. God promises that they will be happy and live long on earth.

3. Children must obey their parents in all things except sin.

4. Children must also obey their teachers and those who have charge of them.

Words to explain for Lesson 30.

Upright: Honest, just.

Avoid: To keep away from.

Escape: To get away.

Complain: To grumble about or find fault with something.

Sometimes on mourning cards or on tombstones, we read the words of hope: "I know that my Redeemer lives and that I shall rise again on the last day." These beautiful words were first spoken by a man very dear to God, named Job. Read the story of Job and find why he spoke these words.

Read Lesson 30

The sayings of Job are full of meaning. Go back over the lesson and review them one by one. Impress some of the thoughts more deeply upon the children by going over them several times and by discussing them more at length. Let them select whichever they like best and memorize them.

Talk especially about patience with and kindness to the old and unfortunate. Have the children tell about some act they have seen in which an unfortunate person or an animal was helped.

Reference to the Apostles' Creed will give the teacher a chance to make these words "The resurrection of the body" more intelligible to the children.

Ruskin's quotation is especially significant at this season of the year. Help the children understand and practice it.

Teacher's References:

The Holy Bible, Gen. xlviii, xlix.

Teacher's Handbook to Bible History, "Jacob's and Joseph's Death," pp. 55–56; "Patient Job," pp. 57–59.

Catholic Action Series, Book II, "Reverence for Parents," "Love for Parents," pp. 292–294.

Teacher's Notes:

Test for Unit II

Twenty-Five is a Perfect Score

I

1. One day God told ......(Abraham)...... to leave Haran and go into the land that He would show him.

2. The land which God promised to Abraham was called the Land of ......(Promise).......

3. The Lord promised Abraham that He would come again

in a year and that by that time Sara, his wife, would have a
...... (son).......

4. Because Lot's wife looked back at the burning city she
was turned into a ...... (statue)...... of ...... (salt).......

5. God remembered His promise to Abraham and Sara and
sent them a little boy whom they called ...... (Isaac).......

6. Abraham sent his servant ...... (Eliezer)...... to the
land of Haran to find a wife for his son ...... (Isaac).......

7. ...... (Rebecca)...... became the wife of Isaac and the
mother of two sons, ... (Esau and Jacob) ....

8. "You shall not be called Jacob any longer," the angel said,
"but ...... (Israel)...... which means 'Strength of God.'"

9. ...... (Joseph)...... was the favorite son of Jacob.

10. The merchants who bought Joseph took him into the
land of ...... (Egypt).......

11. Two years after Joseph had explained the dreams of the
chief ...... (butler)...... and the chief ...... (baker)......
Pharao also had a dream.

12. When the people came to Pharao for food, he said to
them: "...... (Go to Joseph)...... and do all that he shall
say to you."

13. When the famine reached ...... (Chanaan)...... Jacob
sent his ten sons down to ...... (Egypt)...... to buy corn.

14. The silver cup was found in ...... (Benjamin's)......
sack.

15. Joseph said: "It is not by your act that I came here but
by the will of ...... (God)...... who made me ...... (governor)...... of Egypt.

16. "The scepter shall not be taken away from ...... (Juda)
......till He come that is to be sent, and He shall be the
expectation of ...... (nations)...... "

II

Fill in the blank spaces with the right words.

1. Melchisedech took ...... (bread)...... and ...... (wine)
...... and offered it to God.

2. At Mass the priest takes bread and wine and changes it into the ......(Body)...... and ......(Blood)...... of Christ.

3. The first Mass was said on ......(Holy Thursday)......

4. The name of our church is ....

5. In ......(Holy Communion)...... I receive the Body and Blood of Jesus.

6. When we commit a great wrong against God's law it is a ......(mortal)...... sin.

7. When we commit a wrong that is not so great, it is a ......(venial)...... sin.

8. ......(Jesus Christ)...... is the Son of God.

9. There are ......(three)...... persons in God.

10. When we pray we talk to ......(God).......

11. The three things that make a mortal sin are:

    1. ....(The wrong must be very great).

    2. ....(We must know that we are doing a great wrong).

    3. ....(We must fully wish to do the wrong).

12. Jesus Christ gave the power to forgive sins to the ......(Apostles).......

13. The Catholic Church was founded by ....(Christ).....

14. The pope is the visible ......(head)...... of the Church.

15. We bend our knee in church because .....(Christ)..... is on the altar.

16. Jesus comes down from heaven every day during ......(Mass).......

17. The place where we shall always see God face to face is called ......(heaven).......

18. Those who die in mortal sin go to ......(hell).......

19. Those who die in venial sin go to .....(purgatory)......

20. ......(God)...... alone knows and sees everything.

UNIT III

MOSES, THE GREAT LAWGIVER

Time: January and February.

Feasts to Remember

January   6,   Epiphany
                 (Relate this feast to the work of the year. The
                 three wise men have heard the story that a
                 Redeemer would come. They knew about a
                 prophecy that told how a star would announce
                 His coming. At last the star came, and they set
                 out to find the newborn king.)

          21,   St. Agnes

          25,   Conversion of St. Paul

          29,   St. Francis of Sales

February   2,   Candlemas

          3,   St. Blase

          11,   Our Lady of Lourdes
                 (Sing a hymn to Our Lady.)

          24,   St. Matthias, Apostle

The Unit Introduction:

Have the pupils write the different names by which the children of Jacob were known and the reason for each name.

How did the Chosen People come to live in Egypt? For four hundred years they kept their faith in this land of idols, and spoke their own language, which was different from the language of the Egyptians. We can see why they must have been looked upon as strangers in Egypt.

In the last unit we read about some of the great leaders of God's Chosen People. We shall now hear of another great Leader whom God called to the help of His children and learn how he stood by them through all their wanderings for forty years.

Read this introduction once more at the end of the unit and by a few questions recall the chief incidents.

Lesson 31

First Week in January

Aim: The aim of this lesson is to show how and why the children of Israel were oppressed by the Egyptians.

Preparation: If necessary, write the more difficult proper names on the blackboard for drill before the lesson is read. Have the children tell what Joseph did for Egypt. What reward did he and his father get? They were allowed to live in the land of Gessen, which they chose for themselves. Read once more the last two paragraphs on page 100.

Read Lesson 31

Have the children retell the story from the pictures.

A few scenes such as the following may be written for this lesson, and then dramatized by the children. Be sure to let the pupils do their own planning as far as possible.

Scene I. The mother of Moses hears the news that all baby boys must be thrown into the river.

Scene II. The mother and Miriam plan what to do with the baby and get the basket ready.

Scene III. The princess finds the baby in the river and sends Miriam to get her mother. The mother takes charge of her own baby.

Practical Application

Have at least one beautiful picture of Mary bearing the Child Jesus in her arms; also pictures of mothers with their children around them. A variety of simple poems in honor of the Blessed Mother and also a few hymns, would make the work of the week more interesting.

Help the children to plan what they are going to do to show their love for mother when they get home from school. Have them do something very simple, such as going to the store, setting the table, minding the baby, etc. In the morning a remark such as the following will suffice: "I wonder how many remembered to do something special for mother yesterday." It is not well to check up too closely. The children should be left to act voluntarily rather than through any desire to please the teacher.

Let them find little poems of their own in honor of Our Blessed Lady and study a few lines.

Let the children talk about the pictures showing mother-love.

Teacher's References:

The Holy Bible, Exod. ii:i–x.

Teacher's Handbook to Bible History, "The Birth of Moses," pp. 59–61.

Catholic Action Series, "Why We Are Devoted to the Blessed Virgin," p. 255; "Mary, the Catholic Mother," p. 298.

Teacher's Notes:

Lesson 32

Second Week in January

Aim: The lesson shows the call of Moses to be the leader of the Israelites. From God's command that he approach the burning bush with reverence, we may also learn that holy things must be treated with respect.

Preparation: Teach the pronunciation of the new proper names: Mā'dǐán, Jĕth'rō, Aar'on, Hō'rĕb.

Talk about the boy Moses at the court of Pharao. How do you think he felt when he saw the Egyptian masters beating the Jews? What may he have wished sometimes to do?

Read Lesson 32

Notice the goodness and patience of God in dealing with Moses. "I will be with you," He says.

What did Moses mean when he said he was slow and uncertain of speech? Do you know of people who cannot speak very well?

Why was his speech even slower after God had spoken to him? People who talk much to God are often very quiet and do not care to talk much about things that do not concern them.

Practical Application

A "Sacramental Booklet" works out very effectively. If something rather beautiful is desired, silver cutouts on black paper can be used to advantage. The explanation for each article may then be mimeographed on strips of white paper and pasted below the cutout. Rosary beads are easily obtained by means of a paper punch that cuts circular openings. The circular "leavings," or papers cut out by the punch, are used for the beads.

Be sure that the children get the spirit of the devotion in each case. Do not stress the external act at the expense of the underlying devotion.

To the questions at the end of the lesson add as many others as you think necessary for an intelligent understanding of the devotion. (See *Highway to God.*)

Teacher's References:

The Holy Bible, Exod. iii, iv.

Teacher's Handbook to Bible History, "Moses' Flight and Calling," pp. 61–65.

Catholic Action Series, Book II, "Reverence for Sacred Persons and Things," p. 263.

Teacher's Notes:

Lesson 33

Third Week in January

Aim: The story aims to show how God stood by His own people and helped them to get away from the enemy. Just as the Israelites needed God's help, so we, too, need the grace which God gives us for our salvation, especially through the sacraments.

Preparation: Explain the meaning of *plague:* Anything very troublesome and annoying. A punishment thought to be sent by God.

As an approach to the lesson, recall that Moses was appointed by God to lead the Israelites out of Egypt back into the Land of Promise. Why was God watching so carefully over the people of Israel? Who first received the name "Israel"? What had God promised to Jacob (Lesson 17)?

Read Lesson 33

Explain that many things that happened in the Old Testament were like pictures (types) of the New Testament. In this lesson we see the Jews saved by the blood of the lamb. That was a foreshadowing of the Lamb of God, Jesus Christ, who shed His blood to save us.

How do we receive the merits of the blood of Christ? In the form of grace, by means of the seven sacraments.

Practical Application

Review the sacraments in general: the purpose of each sacrament, the necessary preparation, and the special grace received.

When speaking of grace and the sacraments, return again to the story of the plagues, especially the last plague from which the Israelites were saved by the blood of the lamb.

The Church commands us to go to Mass on certain days. However, good Catholics, who understand the great value of the Mass, will not have to be commanded. They will go as often as possible, even on weekdays, to receive the many graces that God offers them.

List the holydays of obligation on the blackboard unless the children already know them well, together with the date. Have the children memorize them.

December 8, Feast of the Immaculate Conception.

December 25, Christmas.

January 1, Feast of the Circumsion.

Ascension Day, forty days after Easter.

August 15, The Assumption.

November 1, All Saints.

The children should know at least what is commemorated on each of these days.

To the questions at the end of the lesson such as the following may be added:

1. Q. What is grace?
   A. Grace is a supernatural gift of God given to us through the merits of Jesus Christ in order that we may save our souls.

2. Q. How many kinds of grace are there?
   A. There are two kinds of grace, sanctifying grace and actual grace.

3. Q. What is sanctifying grace?
   A. Sanctifying grace is that grace which makes the soul holy and pleasing to God.

4. Q. What is actual grace?
   A. Actual grace is help which comes from God to enlighten our mind and move our will in order to keep away from evil and to do good.

5. Q. Can we be saved without grace?
   A. Without the grace of God we cannot go to heaven.

6. Q. Can we refuse the grace of God?
   A. We can refuse the grace of God by not listening to His promptings to do good and avoid evil.

Teacher's References:

The Holy Bible, Exod. vii, xii.

Teacher's Handbook to Bible History, "The Ten Plagues," pp. 65–69.

Catholic Action Series, Book III, "The Frequent Reception of the Sacraments," pp. 36, 37.

Teacher's Notes:

Lesson 34

Fourth Week in January

Aim: The lesson shows how the Israelites, aware of the help of God, crossed through the Red Sea and escaped from their enemies. Aim to teach the children that they too, like the Israelites, should face bravely the little problems of everyday life, knowing that God is their help and strength.

Preparation: Read over the entire lesson and plan the week's work according to the needs and ability of the class. Assign some of the work, such as the stories of the saints, ahead of time. The words, "I Must Be Brave" could be used in the form of a poster or as a motto for the week.

Have the pupils look at the picture on page 120 and repeat what it represents. God had told Moses that after this last plague, the children of Israel would be permitted to leave Egypt. Moses told them to stand ready when the message came for them to go.

Read Lesson 34

Explain "a pillar of cloud by day and a pillar of fire by night." During the day the cloud hid the Israelites from their enemies. At night it lit up the way for them. Give children some sense of the greatness and joyousness of the hymn at the end of the story, by letting them read or chant it in chorus, from the fullness of their own hearts.

I Must Be Brave:

Take each of these sentences individually and, by specific examples from the children's own lives, show what they mean. Take for example the first sentence:

The boys whom Jack goes with, decide one day in spring to go swimming, although they know it is too early in the season, and their parents would not allow them to go. Jack knows the danger. He must be brave and say "No," in spite of the fact that all the others laugh at him and call him a coward. It takes more courage to stand alone than to do what the crowd does. Jack does stand alone as far as the crowd goes, but God is with him, as He was with the Israelites when they crossed the Red Sea.

Using Good Judgment:

1. The aim of this and a number of the following problems is to show that it takes more courage to do the right than to do the wrong. God is with those who are in the right, as we see in our story.

2. Try not only to get the right responses but to influence

the will of the child. If there is to be improvement, there must be a change of mind, of attitude.

3. It may be well also in these problems to discuss the reactions of "the other party." Here, for example, Ray's courage may influence another of the boys to do something similar when the time comes.

4. What if, after the boys offer their apology, the man gives them a sound scolding? They have done their duty, and there is a great deal of satisfaction in that. Furthermore, every time we do a courageous act of this kind we become stronger for one still more courageous.

5. It takes courage to face punishment or even displeasure.

6. Bring out also the good effect her example may have. Perhaps a little story will help.

7. Of course it is all very easy to picture the fine little chap going to help the cripple. The story is brought closer in an actual situation in school when no one is thinking of "problems." It is then that the teacher seizes the opportunity to recall the lesson on courage. It is in this way that character is developed, little by little in the stream of life itself.

8. Discuss each of the three reactions and prove that the simplest, the easiest, and the best way is to be honest.

9. Again weigh each case separately and arrive at the only worth-while conclusion.

More Things for You to Do:

1. These little scenes might be dramatized, or written during language class and used in many other ways. Find a variety of ways to bring out the lesson in question.

2. Choose saints that make an appeal to child life. Catholic readers have a variety of such lives. (See list in Curriculum.)

3. Again, this little story may be worked out in different ways and used for different periods. The class might select the best story to be read before another class, to Sister Superior, to be used in the school paper, etc.

4. The words follow in this order: (*a*) Moses, (*b*) pillar, (*c*) Red Sea, (*d*) Pharao, (*e*) song, (*f*) Aaron.

5. The first quotation is especially worth remembering.

6. It must have been hard for St. Paul to go back after his conversion and tell the Jews that he was mistaken. He knew better than anyone else how full of hatred they were for the Christians.

7. Sing the hymn and then go back to the one the Israelites sang, for the sake of comparison.

The "Good Things to Read" offer splendid material for this lesson.

Can You Answer These Questions?

1. God gave Moses the power to divide the sea.

2. There are three persons in God, the Father, the Son, and the Holy Ghost.

3. We call them the Holy Trinity.

4. Glory to be to the Father, etc. This is a prayer of praise as was the great hymn the Israelites sang. Encourage the children to say it reverently.

Teacher's References:

The Holy Bible, Exod. xiii and xiv.

Teacher's Handbook to Bible History, "The Passage Through the Red Sea," pp. 69–71.

Biblical Questions, "Exodus from Egypt," Chap. XXI, pp. 129–132.

Catholic Action Series, Book I, "The Sacraments of the Holy Ghost," pp. 222–227.

Teacher's Notes:

Lessons 35 and 36

First Week in February

Aim: Lesson 35 aims to show how God, in His goodness, fed the Children of Israel in the desert. It reminds us also that we are fed with the Bread of Life.

Lesson 36 aims to teach us how and when the Ten Commandments were first given by God. We learn at the same time, what these commandments should mean to us.

Preparation: Prepare a short table of sins for each commandment (see Manual for Book III) so that it can be used for a review. Have on hand pictures of the Holy Eucharist, of children receiving Holy Communion, etc. Write under them the words: Manna sent from heaven.

Teach the pronunciation of Mt. Si'naī.

Talk about desert land and why people cannot live in it. What do they lack? Food and water. The children of Israel were happy to get away from their enemy, but they got into a great desert where they wandered around for a long time. Let us see what happened to them there.

Read Lesson 35

Ask questions about the lesson:

Why did food become scarce?

Had the people good reason to grumble?

Should they have known better? Why (from past experience)?

Had God ever helped them before? How?

What should they have done?

Point out especially God's wonderful goodness toward, and patience with, His ungrateful people.

Practical Application

Convince yourself that the children know what and how to pray before and after Holy Communion. Review the directions in Lesson 11, if necessary. It is desirable that Holy Communion be viewed as an integral part of the sacrifice of the Mass. The prayers used by the Church during Mass are the prayers most acceptable as a preparation for Holy Communion. The priest says them in preparation for his Communion, why should not we?

Can You Answer These Questions?

1. The Holy Eucharist is the sacrament which contains the Body and Blood of our Lord Jesus Christ in the form of bread and wine.

2. Christ gave us the sacrament of the Holy Eucharist at the Last Supper.

3. The priest changes bread and wine into the Body and Blood of Christ when he repeats the words which our Lord said at the Last Supper. "This is My Body," etc.

4. Our Lord gave this power to the Apostles and to all bishops and priests who were to come after the Apostles.

5. Bread and wine are changed into the Body and Blood of Christ during the sacrifice of the Mass.

Read Lesson 35 once more in order to get the intimate connection between the Manna which is the type, and the Holy Eucharist, which is the reality.

Read Lesson 36

The Lord wanted the people to realize the importance of the Ten Commandments. Notice how the Israelites had to prepare themselves to receive them.

Explain that the Ten Commandments are meant for us just as much as for the Israelites. They are guideposts on the highway to heaven. If we follow them, we shall not lose our way.

Take this occasion to review the Ten Commandments and those sins against each commandment which the children usually commit. Most of the commandments will be treated again, individually, in different lessons, at which time they may be more thoroughly explained.

This lesson (The Commandments) may be continued through a part of next week.

Teacher's References:

The Holy Bible, Exod. xvi, xvii, xx.

Teacher's Handbook to Bible History, "The Miracles in the Desert," "The Ten Commandments," pp. 71–77.

Biblical Questions, "The Decalogue," pp. 132–137.

Catholic Action Series, Book I, "The Commandments," pp. 131–138.

Teacher's Notes:

Lesson 37

Second Week in February

Aim: This lesson, The Israelites Worship a Golden Calf, shows how willing God is to forgive His people when they confess their fault and do penance. Aim also through this lesson to inculcate the right attitude for and a thorough appreciation of the sacrament of penance.

Preparation: Have on hand a good picture of the Ark of the Covenant. Be sure the pupils understand the two terms, *Tabernacle* and *Ark of the Covenant.*

Tabernacle: A tent used as a place of worship.

Ark of the Covenant: The wooden chest in which the Jews kept the two stone tablets with the Ten Commandments.

In introducing the lesson, speak of the First Commandment and of the promise made by the Israelites that they would keep the commandments God had given them.

Read Lesson 37

What commandment did the people of Israel break? Moses reminded God of the promises He had made to Abraham, Isaac, and Israel. Have the pupils look back for some of these promises. (See pages 30, 31, 47, 60, 99.)

Practical Application

Review the sacrament of penance. Before doing so, use the pre-test at the end of this lesson to find out how much the children already know. It is understood that there is to be no preparation for this test. Devote your time afterward only to those facts which are not yet clear to the class.

Impress upon the minds of the children the fact that confession is good for us not only because it takes away sin, but also because it gives us grace to fight against temptation and to keep away from sin. For that reason it is well to go to confession often.

If the teacher desires to know how well she has put over her instruction on the sacrament of penance, she should give another test including the questions on which most of the class failed in the pre-test.

Retell the story of the golden calf from the picture on page 135.

Pre-Test

This test may be given in order to ascertain what further instruction the pupils need on the sacrament of penance, so that there may be no waste of time on material that has already been mastered by the class.

1. Q. What is the sacrament of penance?
   A. Penance is a sacrament in which the sins committed after baptism are forgiven.
2. Q. Did you ever receive the sacrament of penance? When?
3. Q. What is confession?
   A. Confession is the telling of our sins to a priest to have them forgiven.
4. Q. Who is it that really forgives sins?

A. Christ Himself whose place the priest takes in confession.

5. Q. When and where did Christ give the priest power to forgive sins?

A. When Christ appeared to the Apostles in the Upper Room, after His Resurrection, He said to them: "Whose sins you shall forgive, they are forgiven them; whose sins you shall retain, they are retained." The bishops and priests are the successors of the Apostles.

6. Q. What must we do in order to make a good confession?

A. In order to make a good confession, we must:
   a) Examine our conscience,
   b) Be sorry for our sins,
   c) Make a firm resolution never more to offend God,
   d) Confess our sins to a priest,
   e) Accept the penance which the priest gives us.

7. Q. What kind of sorrow should we always try to have for our sins? Why?

A. We should always try to have perfect contrition for our sins, because it shows that we are sorry because we love God with all our heart.

8. Q. If a person is in danger of death and is in mortal sin, how can he be saved?

A. He can be saved by making an act of perfect contrition with the intention of going to confession if there is a chance.

9. Q. Besides being sorry for our sins, what must we promise God to do?

A. We must promise to amend our lives; that is, to do everything in our power not to sin again; and also to stay away from the occasion of sin.

10. Q. What do you mean by an occasion of sin? Give an example.

A. By an occasion of sin I mean a person, place, or thing that causes us to fall into sin. For example, if we go with a companion who is the cause of our falling into sin, that companion is an occasion of sin for us.

11. Q. What sins must we tell? How many?
    A. We must tell our mortal sins. All of them.
12. Q. If we forget to tell a mortal sin in confession, what shall we do?
    A. We must resolve to tell it in the next confession.
13. Q. What kind of sin would he commit who concealed a mortal sin?
    A. A sacrilege.
14. Q. Are we bound to tell our venial sins?
    A. No, but it is very good for us to do so.
15. Q. What are some of the ways and means of getting rid of venial sins?
    A. Gaining indulgences, doing acts of mercy, offering our sufferings to God for our sins.
16. Q. Why does the priest give us a penance in confession?
    A. In order that we may make up for the temporal punishment due to our sins.
17. Q. When should we say this penance?
    A. Before leaving the church after confession or as soon after as possible.

Chart Results as Follows:

On squared paper write the names of your pupils. Above, number the squares from 1 to 17, one for each question asked in the test. Each number that the pupil has correct is marked with an X in the respective square. When the chart is complete, you will see at a glance which of the questions have been missed by the majority and which by only one or two. Your instructions should be based on the results shown by the chart, in order that there be no waste of time on matter that is already known to the class.

Teacher's References:

The Holy Bible, Exod. xxxii.

Teacher's Handbook to Bible History, "The Golden Calf," pp. 77–79.

Catholic Action Series, Book I, "Sacrament of Penance," pp. 158–168.

Teacher's Notes:

Lesson 38

Third Week in February

Aim: The aim in this lesson is to learn how God punished the spies for their untruthfulness and thereby to impress upon the pupils God's hatred of that sin.

Preparation: The lesson of truthfulness in word and action comes very close to the children. Be sure, however, to use the story as a basis for the work by referring to it frequently. Perhaps some of the little plays may take the form of a puppet show. Bring to your help every possible variety of interests, keeping in mind your aim. Remember, too, that it is not so much what the children say that counts, as how their minds have been impressed with the beauty of the virtue, the necessity and honorableness of truthfulness. In a word, their wills must be incited to right action.

Teach the pronunciation of Cā′lĕb and Jŏs′uē.

Read Lesson 38

Explain the expression "flowing with milk and honey" — rich in fruits and provision of all kinds.

Once before, the people made the same complaint. Have the pupils find the occasion (Lesson 35).

Take note of God's complaint against the people and His ready answer to the prayer of Moses, His great servant. God forgave them their sin but punished them for it. Compare with the eternal and temporal punishment due to sin. God forgives us our sins, but we must still do penance for them.

The quotations might be made in cut-out letters and pasted on a colored background.

What Would You Do?

When possible let the children use the foregoing quotations in answer to these problems.

1. Jean should tell mother what has happened and not let her brother get the punishment. Joe may keep still and not tell on his little sister. He might try to tell her that she should own up and that he will help her bear the blame.

2. Helen may not keep the change. It was not intended for her. She must be honest and return the money.

3. It is not honest for me to let anyone copy, nor is it kind. It is very difficult for people to refuse help of this kind to others. It is really a matter of training the whole group to understand the situation in its proper light. The teacher should know that

Albert cannot work his problems so that she may help him. Albert has a right to an explanation from the teacher. The longer he waits with his difficulty, the harder will it be for him to learn these and related problems.

4. Jane has told a lie by her actions. She knew how mother would understand her. She really intended to deceive her mother and has done wrong.

5. Bob should be prevailed upon to tell that he broke his promise. Of course it would be hard for a little brother to make a big brother do that. Terry should refuse to go along on another occasion to show his disapproval. He need not tell unless he feels that the matter is so serious that the father should know about it. If the boys said nothing and tried it again, the result might be the loss of life. By saying something in time, such a thing could be prevented.

6. Jennie need not hurt Ruth. She can be tactful without being untruthful.

7. Edith is being dishonest because Mrs. Shane has understood that Edith is going to wash the dishes. Someone else may not be as careful about them as Edith. At any rate, Edith has evidently been "hired" to wash them and it is her place to do so or refuse if she cares to.

8. Dave should tell the teacher alone. He has no right to throw suspicion on Sam.

9. A good idea would be to have the leaders of the class persuade the group to acknowledge that they did not deserve her praise. It is a form of dishonesty to make the teacher believe that they were all very good. There is no obligation, however, on the part of the group as a whole, to say more about it.

10. Discuss fully the harm and the good that can be done by the children. Show how foolish talk may spread and cause much heartache and trouble.

11. Joan has another obligation. Since her mother is blaming the grocer for overcharging, she must tell her mother what she did in order not make him lose his trade.

12. Peter is getting books under false pretenses. He is really

dishonest. He knows his mother does not want him to *read* those books and he is doing it anyway. He is just as guilty as if he went to the library to get books after he had been forbidden.

Interesting Things for You to Do:

1. Some of these thoughts could be shown in pantomime with the class guessing what the story is about.

2. When an activity is not directly related to the religion work, it should be used to review the story in order to get the connection. For example, in this case a few sentences should tell where the fruit was found, etc.

Can You Answer These Questions?

1. The Eighth Commandment is: Thou shalt not bear false witness against thy neighbor.

2. Sins against the Eighth Commandment: Lies, rash judgment, backbiting, slander.

3. No, we can lie also by our actions. People who are frequently dishonest in their actions are called hypocrites.

4. If we harm someone by telling a lie we have to try to make up for the wrong we have done.

Teacher's References:

The Holy Bible, Num. xiii, xiv.

Teacher's Handbook to Bible History, "The Spies," pp. 88–91.

Catholic Action Series, Book III, "Truthfulness," pp. 383–384.

Teacher's Notes:

Lessons 39 and 40

Fourth Week in February

Aim: The two lessons show clearly God's displeasure with Moses and Aaron for doubting His word. Aim to have the children understand through these stories that God is still the same and that we have much more reason to hope and trust in God than the Israelites, because He sent us Jesus to teach us to know Him better.

Preparation: Explain: *Doubting:* Not sure whether that will happen which was promised or told.

Teach the pronunciation of: Eleā'zȧr, Mō'ăb, Mt. Nē'bo.

Approach the new lesson by asking questions such as the following:

How did God punish the Israelites who grumbled when the scouts returned from Chanaan?

Did the people have any reason to be afraid? What had God done to show them how He cared for them?

Read Lesson 39

In this lesson we see that even Moses and Aaron doubted God's promise to give His people water from the rock. Their faith was not strong enough the first time the rock was struck.

We, too, must believe all that God tells us.

Practical Application

Explain that a Catholic should say the Apostles' Creed every day. By it we honor God, because we tell Him that we believe all that He has taught us to believe.

The children might make a little "I Believe Booklet" or write sentences in their character books, such as the following (after each article has been simply explained):

I believe in God the Father, Creator of heaven and earth.

I believe in God the Son, who redeemed me.

I believe in the Holy Ghost.

Etc.

Pictures for each article may be placed along the wall and pointed to as the prayer is explained.

Questions such as the following may be asked if desired:

Who teaches us what we must believe?

What great book tells us all about the beginning of the world?

How many persons are there in God?

Etc.

Read Lesson 40

Have the children memorize the words of Moses: "Love the Lord your God with your whole heart, with your whole soul, and with your whole strength."

Ask questions about the lesson.

Why was Moses not allowed to pass into the Promised Land? Did Aaron get to see it? Do you think Moses lost his trust in God because he was punished? How can you tell?

Take a general, oral review of the important events that have been studied so far. Then let the children fill in the blanks. The filling in need not necessarily be done in their textbooks. Let them use a separate sheet of paper and number the answers according to the statements in the text.

Answers: 1. Abraham, Isaac, Jacob. 2. Noe. 3. Moses. 4. Cain. 5. Twenty. 6. Melchisedech. 7. Salt. 8. Isaac. 9. Esau. 10. Rebecca. 11. Israel. 12. Nebo. 13. Famine. 14. Aaron. 15. Ten Commandments. 16. Job 17. Forty. 18. Living creatures, cattle, etc. 19. Sodom and Gomorrah. 20. Manna.

Teacher's References:

The Holy Bible, Num. xxi; Deut. xxxiii, xxxiv.

Teacher's Handbook to Bible History, "The Doubting of Moses and Aaron," pp. 94–96; "Moses' Last Exhortation and Death," pp. 99–101.

Catholic Action Series, Book I, "Preaching the Kingdom of God," Chap. VIII.

Teacher's Notes:

Test Yourself

Which of the Ten Commandments did these children especially remember:

1. Mary broke a vase of which her mother thought very much. She was afraid to tell the truth. The thought came to her that her mother might be made to believe that the cat did it. When her mother asked her about it, Mary said: "I did it, Mother. I am very sorry." (Eighth Commandment)

2. Ed went to the store with another boy. There were some pencils lying on the counter, and when no one was looking, the boy helped himself to a few. Later he took some more and handed them to Ed. Ed would not take them. (Seventh Commandment)

3. Ben went out hiking with a group of boys. At noon they roasted some wieners. Ben remembered it was Friday and did not take any. The boys asked him why he was not eating any sausage. He said: "I am a Catholic." All the boys laughed at him, but he would not eat any of the sausage. Besides keeping the law of the Church, what other commandment did Ben remember to keep. (First Commandment)

4. Ellen was home alone one Sunday. She got up and went to Mass, because she knew that she could adore God best in that way. She spent most of the day reading from a beautiful book about the saints and looking at the colored pictures in the big Bible. In the afternoon she went to devotions. Ellen says that Sunday is always the best day of the week for her. (Third Commandment)

5. Leonard heard a man use the Holy Name in anger. It hurt Leonard to hear the name of God used in that way. He made up his mind that he would never do such a thing. He kept his resolution. (Second Commandment)

6. Ann had just been very ill. After that she was always careful not to get her feet wet or to go out in the cold without her wraps on. She knew that good health is a wonderful gift of God and that He expected her to take good care of it. (Fifth Commandment)

7. Mother told Teresa to stay in the house and watch the baby carefully while she went to town. Teresa's friends called and asked her to come out for a while to play. Teresa said: "I cannot come out to play. Mother is gone and I must watch the baby." (Fourth Commandment)

8. Leo's father called him. Tom said: "Come on, Leo, hide behind the shed. Your father won't know that you are here." But Leo answered, "I don't want to be a hypocrite," and went to see what his father wanted. (Eighth Commandment)

9. May asked Cora to come with her to a movie. May had heard that the picture they would see was not clean. In fact, some of it was so bad that to look at it would cause sinful thoughts. Cora would not go and asked May to stay away, too. (Sixth Commandment)

10. Peter said to Joe: "I dare you to go over there and fight Mike. I bet you can't do it." Peter was bigger and stronger than Mike, and he was not afraid to fight. But he refused to hurt the smaller boy, even if he was dared to do it. (Fifth Commandment)

What is it?

1. A sign by which a Catholic shows his faith? (The sign of the cross)

2. What the priest puts on our foreheads to remind us that our bodies shall return to the earth? (Blessed ashes)

3. The sacramental which is blessed on the Sunday before Easter? (Palms)

4. The sacramental which is blessed on the second of February and must be used at every Mass? (Candles)

5. The sacramental which tells the story of our Lord's suffering and death by means of crosses or pictures? (Stations of the cross)

6. The sacramental which was given to St. Dominic by Our Lady. Should be said every day especially during October? (Rosary)

7. A great hymn of praise sometimes sung in church by all the people at the close of Mass or Benediction? (Te Deum. Holy God We Praise Thy Name)

8. A protection for the Israelites while they were passing through the Red Sea? (Pillar of clouds)

9. Food sent from heaven? (Manna)

10. Laws written on stone tablets and given to Moses on the mountain? (Ten Commandments)

UNIT IV

JOSUE AND THE JUDGES

Time: First two weeks in March.

Feasts to Remember

March 7, St. Thomas Aquinas

17, St. Patrick

The Unit Introduction:

Read the introduction and recall to the pupils' minds either by asking them questions or having them look back for the two events referred to: namely, the first coming to the Land of Promise (Lesson 9) and leaving the Land of Promise (Lesson 28).

Israel is now to be ruled by Judges. When the unit is completed, return to read this introduction again and name the judges mentioned in the lessons.

Lessons 41 and 42

First Week in March

Aim: Lesson 41 shows the Israelites renewing their promise to keep God's Commandments. We, too, have made a promise to God. By means of the story aim to give the children a better understanding of their baptismal vows and encourage them to renew these vows at least once a year.

Lesson 42 shows how God Himself again chose a leader for His people and how this leader willingly accepted the work God intended for him, once he was sure it was His will.

In connection with this story, you might point out how we should also be willing to serve God for the good of others.

Preparation: Approach the new lesson by questions such as

114

the following: How long had the Israelites wandered in the desert? Who was their leader during those forty years? Who was to bring them back into the Promised Land? Were they still far away from the Promised Land when Moses died? How do you know?

Teach the pronunciation of Gĕd'eon, Măd'ïanites.

Read Lesson 41

Note especially the second paragraph. What does it show?

Let the pupils find the lesson in which Jacob adopts the two sons of Joseph.

What were their names? (Lesson 29)

Renewal of Baptismal vows: I renounce Satan, and all his works, and all his pomps, and I pledge myself to Jesus Christ forever.

Can You Answer These Questions?

1. I became a child of the Catholic Church on the day on which I was baptized.

2. Baptism is a sacrament which takes away original sin and all other sins from the soul, makes us Christians and children of God.

3. Baptism frees the soul from all sin and gives it sanctifying grace.

4. I can receive the sacrament of baptism only once.

5. Ordinarily a priest baptizes; but in case of necessity anyone may baptize. The person baptizing should pour water over the head of the one to be baptized and at the same time say the words: "I baptize thee in the name of the Father and of the Son and of the Holy Ghost."

6. The name of a saint is given in baptism in order that the one receiving it may have the saint as a protector and try to imitate his virtues.

More information about baptism may be added by the teacher if desired. For example, the three kinds of baptism: of water, of desire, and of blood.

Review the closing thoughts of the last lesson. When Josue was old, he reminded the people once more of God's goodness to them. Who else had done the same thing before he (Moses) died? What promise did the people make to Josue?

Why did God watch so carefully over His people? How did they know about the Redeemer? Were they always true to God?

Did the people of Chanaan worship the one true God? If you do not recall, look back to Lesson 14.

Read Lesson 42

In paragraph two we see how the Madianites treated the Children of Israel. Why did God permit them to do it?

Notice God's words in the first paragraph on page 155. We have seen often before how clearly God showed His people that He was their help and strength and that without Him they could do nothing. See especially the last part of Lesson 38 for an example.

Practical Application

For the mission activities gather all the material you possibly can, especially pictures and mission magazines. Let the children take charge of the bulletin board and fill it with material referring to the missions. Perhaps, if there is a general school bulletin, they could enlarge their interest to reach the entire school. Make all your plans ahead of time, but remember that the children should have the pleasure of doing the work as far as possible, by making and carrying out their own plans.

Remember also that there is no need of loading yourself with work so as to make the week an extra burden. Make the plans simple enough so that the children will be able to carry on the work by themselves. The "Things to Do" are mostly such activities as can be done without much help on the part of the teacher. Her duty will be principally to create interest and to start them in worth-while activities of their own.

Help the children find something about their patron saints.

In discussing the various ways of being a missionary, give practical examples and keep in mind that one simple little practice well kept is better than too many resolutions made and broken.

Interesting Things for You to Do:

1. Such a poster could be used for the entire school.

2. Warn the children not to carry away from home without permission any magazines the parents may wish to keep.

3. The *Little Missionary* or the list of "Good Things to Read" will furnish material. The stories could be told for oral language work.

5. This can be made a hobby at home. Many a child could be directed to do something worth while during leisure hours, with the wise direction of the teacher.

6. If this activity causes any difficulty, it need not be undertaken.

7. Say a little prayer occasionally in class, but encourage the children to pray of their own accord, also, so that they develop the habit.

8. In some cases the whole family might, in time, be interested.

9. Such work as this can be assigned to a group ahead of time, to save time, so that they are ready for their performance when the occasion comes.

Can You Answer These Questions?

1. God made man to know Him, to love Him, and to serve Him in this world, and to be happy with Him forever in the next.

2. There are many who do not know and love God.

3. Missionaries give up their homes and go to heathen lands because they love God so much that they want as many people as possible to know and love Him.

4. After death the soul goes to heaven, hell, or purgatory.

5. The body is buried and returns to dust.

6. The body will remain in the earth until Judgment Day.

7. The Last Judgment will be at the end of the world. We do not know when that will be.

Teacher's References:

The Holy Bible, Josue iii, iv; Judges vi.

Teacher's Handbook to Bible History, "Entrance into the Promised Land," pp. 101–105; "Gedeon," pp. 106–109.

Biblical Questions, "The Book of Josue," pp. 137–140; "The Book of Judges," pp. 140–142.

Catholic Action Series, Book I, "Your Baptismal Vows," pp. 218–219; "Mission Opportunities," pp. 50–51.

Teacher's Notes:

Lessons 43 and 44

Second Week in March

Aim: Lesson 43 aims to bring out the beauty and dignity of work as shown in the story of Ruth, whose reward was the honor of becoming the great grandmother of David from whose family the Redeemer was finally to come.

Preparation: Teach the pronunciation of Nō'emi, Or'pha, Bō'ŏz, O'bĕd.

This should be an interesting and useful lesson. There are beautiful pictures of Ruth. Talk about them first before beginning the lesson. *The Gleaners* by Millet will fit in very well. Explain what "gleaning" means.

Refer to the famine in Chanaan at the time of Joseph and what the people had to do to get food. Now again we hear of a famine in Chanaan.

Read Lesson 43

Why did Noemi leave Bethlehem?

Look over Lesson 9 and find out where Abraham went during a famine in Chanaan.

The scene between Noemi and her daughters should be dramatized. Be sure to have Ruth use the quoted words in the lesson.

Practical Application

Stress cheerful work especially in the home. In doing so, refer frequently to the lesson in hand. Use the pictures of Ruth and *The Gleaners* to refer to during your discussions. Come back occasionally to the points to be checked. The teacher herself may use some of the points on the written work of the children. For example, a task poorly done may bear the words: "I must do my work well and never be satisfied, etc."

Use stories to illustrate some of the quotations, if there is time. For example: Let someone tell how he earned his first money and how big he felt after earning it himself.

There is no use in having the children write out a great many things they mean to do when they get home. Insist on serious thought and just one or the other little act.

Using Good Judgment:

See how often the children can apply the quotations to these cases.

1. Be careful not to put the children under the impression that one must never play but always do something useful. Play for children is in itself very often purposeful. The aim here is to train children early to find something definite to do whether it be

sewing a doll's dress, reading a book, or sailing a boat in the bathtub. What they should avoid is idleness and dreaming. Encourage good reading. "Be not simply good, be good for something."

2. This problem should help the children to help themselves.

3. She might read, she might straighten things on the counter, or cut out pictures, etc. She should avoid mere idleness.

4. This problem should suggest again to children how much more fun it is to earn a thing oneself than always to depend upon other people to get it for them. Which of the quotations applies?

5. Agnes may not leave the children with others. The lady trusts her but probably does not want anyone else to take care of them. When Agnes accepted the work she really meant to say that she would do it herself.

6. He has no right to his pay. He is dishonest. If he does not want to do the work, he must not offer to do it. It makes no difference whether someone knows about it or not. Children too often are of the opinion, learned from their elders, of course, that as long as they are not caught doing wrong, they are all right. Bring in our duty toward God and the thought that God sees and knows everything.

7. Go back to the points and see what is suggested there.

8. Peggy has a duty. That must be done before she goes to play. Whether the teacher calls for the work or not is not the main consideration.

9. Call for suggestions. Both could, of course, lighten the work of the mother at home by being thoughtful in doing little things for her. Perhaps, occasionally, too, they might run errands for others, etc. The aim is to show that even little children can help and are expected to be a bit thoughtful.

10. If Nan promised that she would take care of it, she should keep her word. Otherwise she should not expect her mother to do the work for her. Which of the points applies?

There is much good reading in the suggested list. Do not forget to bring in St. Joseph's work as a carpenter and our Lord's willing and humble help in the workshop. Show also from the lives of great men how they had to work, often against odds, for example, Lincoln, Edison.

Can You Answer These Questions?

1. On the seventh day of creation God rested.

2. The Third Commandment tells us to keep holy the Sabbath day.

3. The Church forbids people to do hard work on Sundays.

4. No, only manual work, the kind servants usually do.

5. In case of necessity one may do hard work. Give examples.

Lesson 44

Aim: The aim of this lesson is to learn from Samuel to listen attentively to the voice of God within our hearts.

Preparation: If possible, show Van Dyke's picture of the boy Samuel at prayer. Discuss the picture as an approach to the lesson.

Read Lesson 44

Samuel loved to talk to God in prayer. God also talked to him. Because he was always ready to listen to the voice of God, Samuel was chosen as one of the Judges of Israel.

Recall that the Israelites always carried the Ark of the Covenant with them. It was the visible center of their devotion to God. They felt whenever they lost the Ark of the Covenant that they had also forfeited God's pleasure and help.

If you have not done so up to this time, dramatize a scene of a child at night prayers, showing exactly what the child should do, what it should ask itself during the examination of conscience, and what it should do afterwards; for example, asking pardon, etc. In other words, try to establish the habit of evening examination of conscience. Remind the children occasionally of their duty without asking directly who has and who has not omitted the practice.

Can You Answer These Questions?

1. We should examine our conscience every evening before going to bed to find out what wrong we have done during the day.

2. By asking myself what wrong I have done during the day in my thoughts, by my words and by my actions.

3. Before we examine our conscience we should pray to the Holy Ghost to enlighten us that we may know our faults.

Teacher's References:

The Holy Bible, Ruth i, iv; I Kings i–iv.

Teacher's Handbook to Bible History, "Ruth," pp. 111–114.

Catholic Action Series, Book II, "Sanctification of Sunday," Chap. XVIII.

Teacher's Notes:

Test for Unit IV

Find the name below and put it next to the sentence that describes the person.

The brother of Moses. (Aaron)

The man whom God saved from the great flood. (Noe)

The man who sold his birthright to his brother. (Esau)

The daughter of Laban whom Jacob met at the well. (Rachel)

The little boy who said: "Speak, Lord, for your servant hears." (Samuel)

The mother-in-law of Ruth. (Noemi)

The boy who was sold as a slave and became ruler of Egypt. (Joseph)

The beautiful wife of Isaac. (Rebecca)

The high priest who would not punish his wicked sons. (Heli)

The great grandmother of David. (Ruth)

The son of Jacob who was told that the Redeemer would come from his family. (Juda)

The baby boy who was hidden in a basket. (Moses)

The "mother of all the living." (Eve)

The first Judge of Israel. (Gedeon)

The high priest who offered up bread and wine. (Melchisedech)

The patient man who blessed God in spite of all his troubles. (Job)

The boy who was killed by his jealous brother. (Abel)

The father who was willing to sacrifice his only son to God. (Abraham)

The man who became leader of the Israelites after the death of Moses. (Josue)

The youngest son of Jacob (Benjamin)

1. Benjamin	8. Abraham	15. Melchisedech
2. Eve	9. Moses	16. Heli
3. Joseph	10. Rebecca	17. Noemi
4. Aaron	11. Esau	18. Abel
5. Josue	12. Job	19. Noe
6. Gedeon	13. Rachel	20. Samuel
7. Ruth	14. Juda	

UNIT V

ISRAEL RULED BY KINGS

Time: Third week in March to third week in April.

Feasts to Remember

March 19, St. Joseph

(Fosterfather of the Redeemer. St. Joseph, like so many of the Jews who had remained true to God, was waiting and praying for the Redeemer. He had the great happiness of being chosen to become the spouse of Mary, the Mother of the Redeemer, and the foster father of the Redeemer Himself.)

25, The Annunciation

(Review the great Promise made in paradise. Mary is the woman who was to crush the head of the serpent. It is on this day that the angel came to tell her that she would be the Mother of the Redeemer. Take this occasion to review the "Hail Mary" and to resolve to say it with more fervor and understanding. Sing a hymn to Mary.)

Special thoughts on the Passion of our Lord.

Preparation for Holy Week.

The Unit Introduction:

The introduction tells how the Land of Chanaan was divided among the twelve tribes of Israel and how these tribes were governed. Have the pupils look for the names of the two sons of Joseph (Lesson 29).

We come now to a period of Jewish history during which the Israelites were ruled by kings, three of whom we shall hear more about in the following lessons. Return to this introduction once more when the unit has been completed and read it for the sake of getting a more unified picture of it as a whole.

Lesson 45

Third Week in March

Aim: The lesson aims to show how God Himself chose the first king for Israel and also teaches us, through the willing obedience of the Israelites, obedience to and co-operation with civil authority; in a word, good citizenship.

Preparation: Explain the meaning of *anoint* and compare with the anointing during a sacrament, especially Confirmation. Teach the pronunciation of Am'alĕc.

The Israelites saw that other nations were ruled over by kings. They were dissatisfied with the rule of Heli's sons. Why? They came to Samuel to ask that they, too, might be ruled by a king.

Read Lesson 45

Take notice of the fact that Saul was blessed by God while he was obedient; but as soon as he showed himself disobedient and thought he could get along without God, he was no longer happy. Point out that the same holds true with us today.

Explain Samuel's words to Saul in the last paragraph.

Practical Application

Have pictures of the President of the United States, the governor of your state, and other civil authorities posted.

Pictures of Good Citizens, that is, of children who by their conduct are showing themselves as good citizens, should be put on the bulletin board or collected by the children. All in all, make the most of the week to inculcate Good Citizenship from a Catholic point of view, keeping before the children the main interest, namely, the story of the First King of Israel.

The various characteristics of a good citizen may be discussed at length, especially such as have not been taken particularly into consideration up to the present time. The particular needs of the class are, of course, always the first consideration.

These characteristics lend themselves to a variety of exercises, such as spelling, definitions, finding of synonyms, use of the words in sentences, pantomime to illustrate the meaning of each word, posters, etc.

Using Good Judgment:

1. "A good citizen obeys the traffic laws" may be used as a poster theme. Bring home again and again the important point that it is not a question of whether we are being watched or not, but a matter of duty. God expects us, as good Christians, to do our duty. Therefore we do it, whether anyone notices or not.

2. Since the law forbids it, there must be a good reason. What might the reason be?

3. A good citizen does not think of himself alone just as a good Christian does not think of himself alone. We are all members of the same family, of the Mystical Body of Christ. We must love our neighbor as ourselves and should therefore be thoughtful of him.

4. Discuss fire prevention. In this connection it may be well also to point out the thoughtlessness of pulling up wild flowers by the roots and otherwise disfiguring wayside bushes, etc., without regard for beauty or for the enjoyment that others might get out of them.

5. This problem again calls for discussion. Public parks are for everybody to enjoy. A place littered with waste of all kinds is not a place of enjoyment.

6. It is the duty of a good Christian to do unto others as he would have them do unto him. Let the pupils imagine themselves trying to make a little money by selling fruit. What would they expect in a case of this kind? A good Christian does not expect to be rewarded for every little service he renders to others. He acts out of love for God and as a matter of duty. He knows that God sees Him and wishes him to act in this way.

7. Let the pupils go over the list of characteristic traits and tell which of them Maude lacks and why. Above all she lacks honesty, consideration, unselfishness.

8. Stress respect for all authority because authority comes from God. The individual is not so much considered as that for which he stands — the law of the country.

9. Tom was trying to show his love for the flag and all it stands for. Of course a boy might act unreasonably and expose his own life to danger.

10. Find which of the characteristics mentioned Nick lacks.

Interesting Things for You to Do:

2. We are true to ourselves when we are honest with ourselves and do not try to cheat ourselves. A boy cheats himself more than the teacher when he copies a task or tells a lie about his lessons, etc.

3. Since we are stressing conduct in public places, it may be well to select such plays in particular. Too many people have an idea that public property need not be particularly cared for. Show how in the long run the citizens themselves have to pay for all the damage done to public property.

7. The expression "Obedience is better than sacrifices" may have to be brought within the child's experience by means of concrete examples. For example: Marie decides not to drink milk during lent. Her mother says that she needs milk for her health. God will be more pleased with Marie's obedience to her mother than with the sacrifice she would make.

Can You Answer These Questions?

1. God promises those who keep the Fourth Commandment that they will live long and be happy even in this world.

2. We must obey all those who are placed over us, such as our teacher, pastor, anyone who has charge of us, civil authorities, etc.

3. The only time one need not obey those who are his superiors is when the superiors command him to do what is sinful. For example, when the emperors commanded the Christians to sacrifice to false gods, they were not allowed to do so, because God must be obeyed rather than man.

Teacher's References:

The Holy Bible, I Kings ix, x.

Teacher's Handbook to Bible History, "Saul, the First King," pp. 117–120.

Catholic Action Series, Book II, "Authority to Rule from God," pp. 309–317.

Biblical Questions, "Books of Samuel and of Kings," pp. 142–144.

Teacher's Notes:

Lessons 46, 47, and 48

First Week in April

Aim: These three lessons tell about King David from whose house the Redeemer came. There are two specific aims: to teach the children to know and love the psalms, so many of which refer to the Redeemer, and to make them thoughtful of others.

Preparation: Show pictures of King David, especially such as depict him playing the harp. Bring a Bible to school. If the children have become accustomed to handling the Bible, let them find Psalm 22, or any other you may choose, and read a few lines to the class. Show pictures or make posters also of children in the act of cheering others and helping to make them happy. Teach one or the other short psalm set to music. Tie up the lesson with the foregoing one by asking such questions as the following: Who was the first king of the Israelites? Was God always pleased with him? How did God punish him for his disobedience?

Read Lesson 46

Notice particularly the sentence "God sees the heart." It might be used to advantage as a motto. Occasionally the thought may be repeated when a particular situation gives special significance to the sentence.

The spirit of God left Saul, and he became very unhappy. It is the same with us. As long as we remain close to God nothing can really make us unhappy. But when we lose God through mortal sin, we can no longer have peace in our hearts.

Read Lesson 47

Discuss the lesson thoroughly. There are a number of beautiful passages in the story. Note in particular, "You come to me with sword, and spear, and shield: But I come to you in the name of the Lord." Goliath was strong and David comparatively weak; and yet, David won the victory. Why?

Let the pupils discuss David's outstanding characteristics, especially his confidence in God.

Read Lesson 48

Make much of the psalms and of their use by the Church. Call attention to the fact that today at Mass, the priest used parts of psalms as he does every day.

Let the pupils find the quoted passages of the lessons in the Holy Bible.

See whether they can tell what reference the quotations have to the Redeemer.

This would be an opportune time to encourage the singing of beautiful songs and hymns, not only in school but also at home. Let the children often repeat the songs they have learned, so that they will be able to use them at home.

Suggestions for Cheering Others:

Discuss the thoughtfulness of the children mentioned. It will, perhaps, be better not to apply the lessons directly to the class, but rather to let them sink in by themselves as a result of the favorable commendations received by the children. Discuss Problem 6 more fully in order that the children are sure to understand. Ask such questions as the following: "Why did Mollie add the note? Was it good of Mollie to do that? Do you think she should tell any of her friends why she did it? Do you suppose the girls had just as much fun as they would have had with good clothes on? Can you think of anyone who was pleased with Mollie's dealing with the poor girls?"

Problem 7. Discuss Mr. Baker's side of the story. He may be lonely and not want to show it. He may have had a great disappointment in his life, etc.

Can You Answer These Questions?

1. We are on earth to know, love, and serve God, and to be happy with Him forever in heaven.

2. We praise God by prayer, by hymns of praise, by living good lives.

3. The *Gloria,* Holy God, *Laudate Dominum,* Blessed be God, etc.

4. The Second Commandment forbids us to use the name of God in vain.

5. The Second Commandment forbids all false, rash, unjust, and unnecessary oaths, blasphemy, cursing, and profane words.

Explain the difference between cursing and swearing if the children do not know; also try to make clear to some extent what is sin and what is not when using the name of God.

Teacher's References:

The Holy Bible, I Kings xvii.

Teacher's Handbook to Bible History, "Goliath Challenges Israel," "David Anointed as King," pp. 120–124.

Catholic Action Series, Book II, "God's Care for Those Who Live by the Law of Love," pp. 424–426; Book I, "Thou Shalt Love Thy Neighbor as Thyself," pp. 266–275.

Teacher's Notes:

Lesson 49

Second Week in April

Aim: To hear of the wisdom of Solomon, son of David, and therefore forefather of the Redeemer, and from him to learn to choose wisely in the various situations in life.

Preparation: Children may have the wrong conception of the word "wise" since it is so often used in the sense of "smart" or "sly." Make sure that they get the true sense of the words "wisdom" and "wise" as used in this lesson. By way of approach to the lesson, you might tell the children to think of something they would ask for if the Lord told them to make a choice. King Solomon was asked to do something similar. What do you think he asked for? Let us see from the lesson.

Read Lesson 49

Point out God's generosity in answering the prayer of Solomon. God is never outdone in generosity.

Make sure that the pupils understand how Solomon knew who was the mother of the living child.

It may be well to mention that Solomon did not remain as good a king as he might have been. He did not always make use of the grace God had given him.

Make a Wise Choice

1. Discuss the wisdom of choosing the proper food. Perhaps you can show what the difference might be in the health of the child who chooses food wisely and one who eats whatever is most to his taste.

2. The aim here is to show that a poor person ought to think twice before spending money foolishly. Often it is just such conduct as Elmer's that makes and keeps people poor. They are not wise enough to lay aside a bit for something worth while. Elmer might save all or at least some of the money. He might learn to spend wisely and still get a great deal of more lasting pleasure than from a movie of the kind he went to see.

In such problems as these be careful, however, not to put the children under the impression that they are always expected to do the hard and disagreeable thing. Much depends upon the attitude you take. It might be shown what great fun it would be for Elmer to start a library all his own at home and to select the books that are going to be very dear to him all his life. Or, how he could surprise mother some day, when she is in great need, by telling her he had saved some money of his own and could help her out, etc.

3. Discuss the relative need for a party dress and a coat and the use and comfort that result from the coat.

4. Have the pupils point out the various results of the delay.

5. Show how Millie is cheating herself more than her mother, etc.

6. This gives you an opportunity to point out that older people know better than children what is good for them. Recall "Robin's Disobedience," page 74.

7. Picture Rose having to give up reading altogether after a short time, because of her disobedience; whereas, if she is wise and listens to the doctor's advice, she may be able to enjoy the use of her eyes all her life.

8. Polly is too young to be a good judge. Older people know from experience that it is harmful to get wet feet. Picture again, Polly happy and healthy, because she has been careful of her health, and on the other hand, Polly sickly, unable to enjoy the many pleasures of childhood.

9. Ed really has to make a difficult choice, but he must choose wisely. Try to apply the situation intimately to cases of their own.

10. Point out the various difficulties that will arise as a result of Jack's not doing the right thing. Boys make much of being courageous. It takes much courage to face a punishment such as awaits Jack.

11. You have again here a case of proving that in the long run Dot hurts no one so much as herself. She will be the loser and no one else.

12. The one meal will appeal more, perhaps to the children,

the other will have far better results for them. It is well for the pupils to give these matters serious thought. Make it such an exercise rather than a guessing game.

Talk over the sayings of King Solomon. They should be memorized and used often. If you desire, let the pupils find more in the Bible (Book of Wisdom). It is well to let the children see for themselves how many wonderful things can be read directly from the Bible, even if they are too young to appreciate them fully. You are at least building up a general attitude of appreciation and reverence for the Holy Bible which will bear fruit in later years.

Can You Answer These Questions?

2. Thou shalt not kill.

3. The sins against the Fifth Commandment are: willful murder, fighting, anger, hatred, revenge, and bad example.

If desired, dwell on this commandment more at length.

Teacher's References:

The Holy Bible, III Kings iii.

Teacher's Handbook to Bible History, "Solomon's Prayer and Wise Decision," pp. 139–141.

Catholic Action Series, "Catholic Action and Leisure," Chap. X, especially pp. 402–405.

Teacher's Notes:

Test for Unit V

I

See how many of these blanks you can fill out without using your book.

1. For two years ......(Saul)...... led the people to victory over the Philistines, and God was with him in every battle.

2. (Obedience)...... is better than sacrifices.

3. The spirit of the Lord left Saul and came upon ...... (David)......

4. Saul's son ......(Jonathan)...... also learned to love ......(David)...... and the two promised to be true friends as long as they lived.

5. (David)...... said: "You come to me with sword, and spear, and shield: But I come to you in the name of the Lord." Then he ran to meet ......(Goliath)......

6. The word ......(psalm)...... means a song that was formerly sung to the music of a harp.

7. David lived about ......(1000)...... years before the Redeemer was born.

8. And ......(Solomon)...... answered: "Give me, O Lord, an understanding heart, so that I may be able to judge Your people and to tell good from evil."

9. (Samuel)...... took the horn filled with oil and anointed David king of Israel.

10. We know that Jacob had ......(twelve)...... sons. Each of these became the forefather of a large group of people known as a ......(tribe)......

11. But the tribe of ......(Levi)...... were not given any land because they were priests.

12. Solomon built a beautiful ......(temple)...... to the Lord and made the country more powerful than ever.

II

Answer the following questions:

1. What is a sacrament? (A sacrament is an outward sign instituted by Christ to give grace)

2. Which is the sacrament we must receive first? (Baptism)

3. What is the Holy Eucharist? (The sacrament which contains the Body and Blood of Jesus Christ under the appearances of bread and wine)

4. What sacrament makes us soldiers of Christ? (Confirmation)

5. What is the sacrament called that makes a man and woman husband and wife? (Matrimony)

6. Who can receive the sacrament of holy orders? (Any Catholic man who is properly qualified)

7. What sacrament should one receive when in danger of death? (Extreme Unction)

8. In what sacrament is sin forgiven? (Penance)

9. How often can confirmation be received? (Only once)

10. When must the sacrament of penance be received? (At least once a year)

11. Which sacrament should be received daily if possible? (Holy Eucharist)

12. How often can baptism be received? (Only once)

13. Who gave us the commandments? (God)

14. What commandment forbids us to harm our bodies? (Fifth Commandment)

15. What is the Second Commandment? (Thou shalt not take the name of God in vain)

16. What promise does God make in the Fourth Commandment? (Long life to those who honor father and mother)

17. What commandment tells us to keep the Sabbath holy? (Third Commandment)

18. What commandment forbids us to take what does not belong to us? (Seventh Commandment)

19. What is the Eighth Commandment? (Thou shalt not bear false witness against thy neighbor)

20. What commandment tells us to keep pure in mind and body? (Sixth Commandment)

21. What commandment did Cain break? (Fifth Commandment)

22. What commandment did the Israelites break when they adored a golden calf? (First Commandment)

23. What commandment do they break who curse and swear? (Second Commandment)

24. What commandment do they break who grieve and disobey their parents? (Fourth Commandment)

25. What happens every time we break a commandment willfully? (We commit sin)

UNIT VI

GREAT PROPHETS OF ISRAEL

Time: Third week in April to second week in May.

Feasts to Remember

April 29, St. Mark, the Evangelist
(Wrote one of the four Gospels. Have the pupils look up a quotation from the Bible, such as Mark viii. 36 and 37. Remember that the aim is to familiarize the pupils with the Bible and those who wrote it.)

May   1, SS. Philip and James, Apostles
(St. Philip was crucified. St. James, known as the Less, was thrown from the temple and killed. What color vestment will the priest wear at Mass? Why?)

May   3, Finding the Holy Cross
(Tell something of the story. Who foretold that the hands and feet of the Redeemer would be pierced? Find words in Lesson 48.)

May   4, St. Monica
Second Sunday after Easter
(Speak of the Gospel of the Good Shepherd. Have the pupils look for it in the Bible. John xxii. 16. Come back to this Gospel when you read Lesson 56.)

The Unit Introduction:

Read the introduction with the class. We have already met with one prophet, the great King David. David is called a prophet because he foretold a great deal about the Redeemer. What were some of the things he foretold? What were the songs called, in which David sang about the Redeemer?

Arouse special interest in those words of the prophets which tell about the Redeemer. Show by example, what it means to foretell an important event. Suppose I were to say that in the year 2000 a great man is to come into the world, and that I would tell also what his name will be, and what great things he will do for the world. Suppose I wrote down all these things and in the year 2000 people would find my words and say: "Just think! This person knew more than sixty years ago what was going to happen! He is a prophet! The prophets of the Old Testament foretold what was going to happen, five hundred, seven hundred, and even a thousand years before the Redeemer really came.

Read the introduction again at the end of the unit and in the light of the newly acquired knowledge review the more important thoughts.

Lessons 50 and 51

Third Week in April

Aim: The lesson aims to show how the Lord proved Himself the true God through His great prophet Elias and how foolish were the superstitious beliefs of the idolatrous people.

Preparation: Teach the pronunciation of proper names: Eli'ăs, Sărĕph'tà, A'chăb, Bā'ăl, Elĭsē'us.

In the lesson of this week we see how far some of the Chosen People had turned away from God. But in His great mercy God sent the prophets to preach to the people and bring them to their senses. We shall now hear about the prophet Elias and see the work that God did through him for the good of the superstitious Israelites. Lesson 51 should take the greater part of the time allotted for the week. In fact, if you find that you would like to use more time for the lesson, carry it over into the next week or have the reading done during a reading period in order to gain time for the important discussions. As the faults considered in these two lessons are common among children, you should make a particular effort to form the right attitude of mind in their connection.

Read Lesson 50

Call attention to the simple faith of Elias and again of the widow of Sarephta.

Why did Elias tell the prophets of Baal to call louder?

Why did he put water all around his altar and also have it poured over the bullock?

What happens to the earth when no rain falls for a long time?

Why do you think the rain came now?

Aim to get children to understand the difference between superstition and a simple, childlike faith. Elias believed all that God told him. The people foolishly thought that Baal could help them. We believe what God and the Church teach, because God is truth and He directs the Church so that she cannot err.

Can You Answer These Questions?

1. Idolatry means the giving to a creature the honor which belongs to God alone.

2. The First Commandment forbids idolatry.

3. Other sins committed against the First Commandment are sins against faith, hope, and charity. We sin against faith: (1) by not trying to know what God has taught, (2) by refusing to believe all that God has taught, (3) by neglecting to make known our belief in what God has taught. We sin against hope by presumption and despair. (Teach by practical examples.) We sin against charity or the love of God by all sin, especially mortal sin.

5. Catholics do not adore the Blessed Virgin and the saints but honor them because they are the special friends of God.

6. The saints can help us by praying to God for us.

Prepare the words for Lesson 51: Nā'ámăn, Jĕr'ĭchō, Bĕth'ĕl, Sy'rĭă, chided.

Read Lesson 51

Let the children make their comments on various parts of the lesson.

The first paragraph should impress upon the children the fact that God will not have those who serve Him mocked. Priests and Sisters are especially devoted to the service of God just as

Eliseus was. They should always be careful to say only what is good about them. Often we do not appreciate the many favors and graces we receive through our wonderful faith. Like Naaman we turn away. If, for example, there were only one place in the world where Mass was being said and Christ could be received in Holy Communion, how eager we would all be to go to that place and be able to have so great a privilege.

Note also how the servant of Eliseus was punished for his dishonesty.

Practical Application

In the last lesson we learned about the First Commandment. If you have not dwelt particularly on the devotion to the saints and the reasons why such a devotion is not the same as idolatry, do so now. Use the lesson about Elias as an illustration. It would be interesting for the children to find out from the pastor what relics are in the altar of your church. The purpose of such relics on the altar could also be told them briefly, or perhaps, mentioned by the Reverend Instructor. This will help them understand better and appreciate more, the great mystery of the Holy Sacrifice.

Using Good Judgment:

Since faults against the Seventh Commandment are common among children and often so serious in their bearing upon character, do all in your power to get them to think seriously about them. Remember, it is not so much what they answer but what attitude they take afterwards, that is important.

Get the children over the idea that as long as a sin is not a mortal sin there is not much harm done. While a mortal sin, being a serious offense against God, is the greatest evil, children must remember also that the effect of *all* sin upon themselves is a serious matter. Drawing the line between venial and mortal sin, just "getting by" by the skin of their teeth, so to say, shows a wrong attitude toward God. Stress rather the other side: God is so good, He desires us to keep all His commandments. Are we going to hurt Him? Are we going to say, "Oh, well, as long as I don't lose my soul, I don't care so much whether I offend God or not"?

1. Lost articles are not ours. They must be returned. We must do all we can to find the owner. Naturally the one who finds the article, has the first right to it, if the owner cannot be found.

2. While Buddy has not the intention to steal, he is forming a very bad habit that may lead to stealing.

3. Eva has no right to the ten cents she received as change. She must return it to Mrs. Mills.

4. By this time the children should be able to take notice not only of the act itself, which is, of course, wrong, but also of the consequences upon the character of Roger. Both Roger's brother and sister do wrong; the one by encouraging him in his sin, the other by keeping silence when she should speak. The case would be different, of course, were the sister very much younger and hardly able to influence Roger.

5. Leo has no right to help himself. If the grocer really does not care, why does not Leo ask for the things he wants? He is forming bad habits which are only too common among children and which must be checked not so much because of the seriousness of the matter itself as because habits are formed "by unseen degrees."

6. The money belongs to the church. The two girls have no right to it. They must return the money and when they confess their sin, tell that they took it from church, because that makes the sin more serious.

7. Dick is accepting stolen goods and is as guilty as the thief himself. He should tell the teacher or some other responsible person, so that they can stop Paul before it is too late. He must be careful not to tell anyone else.

8. Unless you know that your parents intend them to be given away, you must ask. They may be valuable to someone and you have no right to them without asking, even if they are from your own home. (There is not always a question of sin, as you will notice, but rather a question of right conduct: it is the right thing to do, the children should reason; God wishes me to do the right thing. Therefore I shall do it.)

9. Margaret is responsible for the damage done and must tell Ann about it. If possible she should have the skates repaired herself.

10. If both did an equal amount of work, it is only fair that the money should be divided equally, since Mr. Roy intended it for both. By keeping the money for himself Matt does an injustice to Arthur.

Can You Answer These Questions?

1. The First Commandment is "I am the Lord thy God: Thou shalt not have strange gods before Me."

2. The First Commandment does not forbid us to pray to the saints. We do not adore the saints but ask them for their help. It is God who gives them the power to hear and help us.

3. The highest among the saints is the Blessed Virgin Mary.

4. A relic is a part of the body of a saint or of objects directly connected with saints.

5. Yes, a Catholic may honor a relic just as we honor objects that belonged to someone very dear to us.

7. I may not keep what I find. I must try my best to find the owner.

8. I must return them and confess the sin.

Teacher's References:

The Holy Bible, IV Kings ii, v.

Teacher's Handbook to Bible History, "The Prophet Elias," "The Sacrifice of Elias," pp. 149–154; "The Prophet Eliseus," pp. 158–159.

Biblical Questions, "Elias and Henoch," pp. 144–145.

Catholic Action Series, Book II, "Superstitions," pp. 259–263; "Honesty," Chap. XXIII.

Teacher's Notes:

Lesson 52

Fourth Week in April

Aim: The aim of this lesson is to learn from Tobias how the love of God expresses itself in good works.

Preparation: Words to learn: Assyr'ïäns, Tobi'as.

Swallow: a bird. (Show picture, if possible.)

Corporal works: Those done for the body.

Spiritual works: Those done for the soul.

Have ready the spiritual works of mercy to read to the children.

We have heard much about the idolatrous Israelites and how they often turned away from God. But there were good people, too, who always tried to do the right thing. We shall hear about one of these today.

Read Lesson 52

Explain why the Israelites were so particular about burying their dead. What sentence in the lesson of Job explains this ("I know that my Redeemer lives and that I shall rise again on the last day")?

Let the children tell how they can apply to their own lives the advice Tobias gave to his son.

Explain, simply, the Mystical Body of Christ. We are all members of the same body, parts of the same body, Christ being the head. Therefore we should help one another and love one another just as we would care for the different parts of our own body. If our eyes pain, the hands do all they can to help them. When our head aches the whole body seems to suffer along. It should be the same with the Mystical Body.

The Corporal Works of Mercy could be easily dramatized or worked out into a series of little plays that would lend themselves very well to a program for the parents, the P. T. A., etc.

The children should be taught to live what they learn, here and now, and not be satisfied with dreaming of the wonderful things they are going to do by and by. In other words, while their little practices should always be easy and simple and in a sense interesting for them, the pupils should be encouraged to do something definite and do it as soon as possible. They must never, of course, burden themselves with all kinds of practices. Their desire to do little things like those suggested, should be the natural consequence of their conviction, their attitude toward their neighbor, etc.

Interesting Things for You to Do:

1. Tell not only which they can do, but also just in what particular instance they can do it. Not only "I can feed the hungry" but, "the next time I see a poor boy or girl, perhaps I can get a chance to slip him an apple or a cookie without making a big fuss about it or having anybody else see me."

2. The children should be encouraged throughout to take their little problems home and get the parents' interest and co-oper-

ation, without being troublesome to them. Preferably, let them tell what acts of kindness they have seen others do.

3. If you have time, explain some of these works to the children as you read them.

4. Encourage the children to copy what they will want most to remember for themselves.

5. Perhaps you can let them choose one particular act and write a story about it during language class.

6. Abraham, Rebecca, Daughter of Pharao, Ruth, etc.

Can You Answer These Questions?

1. Everybody is our neighbor.

2. We should love our neighbor because he is a child of God like ourselves, a member of the same family, of the Mystical Body of Christ.

3. We can show our love for our neighbor by doing him good, by wishing him good, by praying for him (by means of the corporal and spiritual works of mercy).

Teacher's References:

The Holy Bible, Tob. iv.

Teacher's Handbook to Bible History, "Advice of Tobias to His Son," pp. 165–166.

Catholic Action Series, Book I, "Corporal Works of Mercy," pp. 271–273.

Teacher's Notes:

Lessons 53, 54, and 55

First Week in May

Aim: The story of Tobias accompanied by his angel aims to show God's loving care for those who served Him faithfully and also to increase devotion to our Guardian Angels. Lessons 54 and 55 aim to bring before the children two of the great prophets and some of their prophetic sayings, particularly about the Redeemer.

Preparation: Teach the pronunciation of: Rā′gĕs, Găb′elus, Ti′grĭs, Ràgu′ĕl, Răph′aĕl.

Fish Gall: a small sack filled with a bitter fluid, found in the body of the fish.

We learned in the last lesson how faithfully Tobias served God. We have often seen, too, how willing God is to help those who love and serve Him. In our lesson for today we shall hear how God rewarded the good works of Tobias.

Read Lesson 53

Have the pupils point out throughout the lesson, the many gracious acts of the angel. The angel stood all prepared for the journey and showed himself ready to go with Tobias. He promised he would bring Tobias back again to his parents. He told Tobias to pull out the fish, and keep the gall, etc.

Repeat parts of the story with the pupils by talking about the picture on page 208.

Be sure to use the last part of the story and especially the quoted words for dramatization. The scene could close with a hymn to the Guardian Angel.

Make at least one day an "Angel Day." If necessary do some of the work you may plan during another period, for example, the reading period, the language period, etc. In a word, let as much of the activities ·of the day as possible center around the angels.

Have pictures of angels on the bulletin board and have children find as many as they can themselves.

Interesting Things for You to Do:

3. Have the children also recall other occasions when angels appeared, for example, on Christmas night, etc.

4. These should be living pictures. While they are being posed for, sing a hymn or recite a poem to fit into the picture. Let the children use their own ingenuity.

Can You Answer These Questions?

1. The angels are pure spirits made by God.

2. They are in heaven face to face with God and also on earth doing the will of God.

3. The angels protect us and help us to be good.

4. Not all the angels remained good. Some of them disobeyed God and were thrown into hell.

5. The angels that disobeyed God are called devils.

Teach the pronunciation of the following words for Lesson 54: Isă′ias, Emmăn′ūĕl, Counselor.

Explain:

Sepulcher: grave.

Persecute: to treat badly; to do harm again and again.

Resurrection: arising from the dead.

In preparation for the lesson on Isaias, have the pupils recall all that they have learned so far, about the Redeemer. Dwell especially on the promise in paradise, on Jacob's promise to Juda and on David's prophecies.

Read Lesson 54

Make the most of the wonderful prophecies of Isaias. Take them one by one and see just what each tells us in particular and how it applies to the Redeemer. Have the pupils listen for the words *Agnus Dei* at Mass. Explain why the Redeemer was compared to a lamb. Find symbols showing a lamb representing Christ. Look for these symbols in your own church.

Teach the pronunciation of the following words for the next lesson: Jĕremi'as, Băb'ylŏn, Nabuchodonō'sor.

Recall to the pupils in preparation for this lesson, that the prophets were sent to bring the people back to God.

Read Lesson 55

Notice the warnings of Jeremias and his great sorrow for the stubborn people. Try to impress the children with the great pride the Israelites had in their capital city, Jerusalem, with its glorious temple. Who built the first temple in Jerusalem? (Solomon)

The words of Jeremias, "O all you that pass by the way, attend and see, if there be any sorrow like to my sorrow" are often found under pictures and statues of the Sorrowful Mother. See whether the pupils can tell why.

Answers to Questions · About the Redeemer:

1. The Redeemer was promised for the first time in Paradise.

2. God felt sorry for Adam and Eve because heaven was closed through their sin and they and their children had no way of opening it.

3. Abraham, Isaac, Jacob, David.

4. Isaias.

5. Ruth.

Interesting Things for You to Do:

If the children have a character book they might add a picture of a lamb and write under it the invocation "Lamb of God, who takest away the sins of the world."

Teacher's References:

The Holy Bible, Tob. v, x.

Teacher's Handbook to Bible History, "Tobias and the Angel Raphael," pp. 166–168; "The Prophet Isaias," pp. 169–171; "Captivity at Babylon," pp. 173–175.

Biblical Questions, "Christ in Prophecy," pp. 168–177.

Catholic Action Series, Book I, "The Prophets Foretell Christ," pp. 82–85.

Teacher's Notes:

Test for Unit VI

I

Tell who said these words:

1. And they gave Me gall for My food, and in My thirst they gave Me vinegar to drink. (David, Ps. 68)

2. Behold, a virgin shall conceive and bear a son and His name shall be called Emmanuel. (Isaias)

3. The scepter shall not be taken away from Juda, till He come that is to be sent and He shall be the expectation of nations. (Jacob)

4. His sepulcher shall be glorious. (Isaias)

5. I shall place enmities between thee and the woman, and thy seed and her seed: she shall crush thy head, and thou shalt lie in wait for her heel. (God in paradise)

6. They have dug My hands and My feet, they have numbered all My bones. (David, Ps. 21)

7. He was offered because it was His own will, and He opened not His mouth. (Isaias)

8. He shall come down like rain upon the fleece; and as showers falling gently upon the earth. (David, Ps. 71)

9. O all you that pass by the way, attend and see if there be any sorrow like to my sorrow. (Jeremias)

10. A child is born to us, and a son is given to us, and the government is upon His shoulder. (Isaias)

II

Finish the quotation by putting in the missing words:

1. Do unto others as you would have them ...... (do unto you).

2. In the beginning God created ...... (heaven and earth).

3. (Lost time) ...... is never found again.

4. It is better to be ...... (alone than in) bad company.

5. (Blessed are the meek,) ...... for they shall possess the land.

6. All obedience worth the name must be ...... (prompt and ready).

7. The fear of the Lord is the beginning of wisdom. Fools ...... (despise wisdom and instruction).

8. The world is so full of a number of things
I'm sure ...... (we should all be as happy as kings).

9. My strength is as the strength of ten
Because ...... (my heart is pure).

10. My son, hear the instruction of thy father, and ...... (forsake not the law of thy mother).

11. I know that my Redeemer lives and that ...... (on the last day I shall rise again).

12. The harder we have to work for something, the more we ...... (enjoy it when we get it).

13. And they gave Me gall for My food, and ...... (in My thirst they gave Me vinegar to drink).

14. Everyone who does the best he can ...... (is a hero).

15. Do not turn away your face from the poor and the Lord ...... (will not turn His face away from you).

16. Fear God and keep ...... (His commandments).

17. An honest man is the ...... (noblest work of God).

18. Share your bread with the hungry and poor and cover ...... (the naked with garments).

19. (Work hard) ...... pray hard, play hard.

20. A good name is ...... (better than riches).

UNIT VII

THE BABYLONIAN CAPTIVITY

Time: Second week in May to first week in June.

Feasts to Remember

May 15, St. John Baptist de la Salle
25, St. Gregory VII
26, St. Philip Neri
31, St. Angela Merici

The Unit Introduction:

Read the introduction and talk about it. Why did God send the prophets? What were some of the things they told about the Redeemer? What else did they tell the Jews? What king took away the people to Babylon? Do you think the Jews liked to stay in Babylon? What was there in their own country that they were especially proud of? In the picture on page 216 (text) we can see the Children of Israel weeping at the thought of their own country and the beautiful temple in which they worshiped God. In this unit we shall learn how good God was to His people even after all their wickedness, and how He helped and consoled them in captivity.

Be sure to let the children memorize the beautiful Scripture text.

Come back to this introduction once more after you have completed the unit and have the class tell how God showed that He still loved His sinful people.

Lessons 56 and 57

Second Week in May

Aim: Lesson 56 aims to show again the great love and mercy of God for the people whom He had chosen as His own and who had so often forsaken Him. Lesson 57 aims to teach that we must obey God more than man, even as Daniel did at the risk of his own life.

Preparation: Teach the pronunciation of proper names: Ezĕ′chĭĕl, Hăb′ăcuc.

Have one of the pupils prepare to tell the story of the Good Shepherd. Show pictures of the Good Shepherd and also of Daniel in the Den of Lions.

Recall to the minds of the pupils that the Chosen People had been taken away from their land by Nabuchodonosor as Jeremias had foretold. Look at the picture on page 216. The Israelites were homesick and discouraged. God had pity on them. We shall see how He renewed their hope and courage once more.

Read Lesson 56

In discussing the first paragraph, recall to the pupils' minds that it was the duty of the prophets to bring the people back to God, to remind them of His mercy, and to keep up their faith and courage.

Ezechiel must have prayed much for his people and begged God to bring them back to their beloved Jerusalem. God rewarded his prayers by a wonderful vision. The promise made by God shows beautifully His great love for His people. It is well worth memorizing.

Recall again the words of Job: "I know that my Redeemer lives, and that on the last day I shall rise again." Note especially the words of mercy spoken by God. Read them again slowly for the class that they may get some impression of their beauty and tenderness.

Can You Answer These Questions?

1. The soul after it is judged by God goes either to hell, to heaven, or to purgatory.

2. The body is put in the grave.

3. The body will arise again on the last day.

4. Hell is the place where the devils are and where the souls of the damned are punished forever by being separated from God.

5. Heaven is the place we see and enjoy God face to face.

6. Purgatory is the place where the souls of the dead are cleansed from venial sin and temporal penalties before they can enter heaven.

7. We can help the souls in purgatory by praying for them, by doing good works for them, and by gaining indulgences for them.

If desired, speak here also of the Particular and the Last Judgment and of temporal and eternal punishment due to sin.

When a person dies, his soul appears before the Great Judge and receives its sentence either for heaven, purgatory, or hell. On the Last Day all the good and all the bad are called together for the Last Judgment. After that there will be no more purgatory. The good will all go to heaven together and the bad will all go to hell.

Read Lesson 57

We see again how God protects those who love and serve Him.

In connection with this lesson show more at length the great evil that sin is. Daniel was willing to be devoured by lions rather than give up his faith in the one true God. It was sin that sent our first parents out of paradise and closed heaven. It was sin that created hell. It is sin that keeps us away from God. It was sin that crucified the Son of God because it was from sin that He came to redeem us. What a terrible thing sin must be, to cause all the misery and sufferings of this world.

If you have succeeded in creating the right atmosphere for a real detestation of sin and its consequences, stop to make a sincere act of contrition with the class.

Through Daniel's courage and fidelity, the king and many of his people came to believe in the one true God. Let the children talk about the picture.

Interesting Things for You to Do:

1. As the story is told, be sure to bring out the thought that these martyrs obeyed the law of God more than that of men, just as Daniel did.

Correlate here the petition of the Our Father, "Deliver us

from evil." The only real evil is sin. Let us think of this when we say the Our Father, and mean it with all our heart when we beg of God to keep away from us all sin.

Can You Answer These Questions?

1. Sin (that is, actual sin) is a willful thought, word, deed, or omission against the law of God.

2. We commit sin when we know and understand that what we are doing is wrong and then still do it because we want to.

3. We can commit sin in our thoughts, in our words, and in our actions.

4. When the matter is important, we commit a mortal sin.

5. Through mortal sin we lose our souls, if we do not repent.

6. We can keep away from sin by prayer, by staying away from bad companions and other occasions of sin, and by learning to overcome ourselves through mortification and self-denial.

7. As soon as we have committed a mortal sin, we should make a good act of contrition and then go to confession as soon as possible.

Review also, if desired, original sin, the effects of venial sin, temptation, the necessity of frequent reception of Penance and the Holy Eucharist.

Teacher's References:

The Holy Bible, Ezech. xxxvii; Dan. i, xiv.

Teacher's Handbook to Bible History, "The Jews on Babylon," "Ezechiel's Vision," pp. 175–176; "The God Bel," "Daniel in the Lions' Den," pp. 183–184.

Catholic Action Series, Book I, "The Resurrection of the Body," pp. 256–257.

Teacher's Notes:

Lesson 58

Third Week in May

Aim: The aim of the lesson is to show how the beautiful Queen Esther came to save her people, the Chosen People, still watched over tenderly by God. It also teaches us that we, too, can become of great use to our country, if, like Queen Esther, we try also to serve God with all our hearts.

Preparation: Teach the new words: Mär'dochai, Assuë'rus, A'măn.

Gibbet: A wooden framework, used to hang people.

At last the years of captivity were over. Many of the Jews returned to their own country. When we remember that most of them must have been born in exile, we can easily imagine that some did not wish to leave, even though they were free to go. Then some wicked man who hated the Jews, planned to have them all killed. How they were saved by a beautiful queen is told in our next story.

Show pictures of the much-loved heroes and correlate little stories, poems, songs, of a patriotic nature with the religion work of the week, always showing or, preferably, inferring that a good Catholic loves his country and is an asset to his country.

Read Lesson 58

Discuss the lesson and the picture with the children. There is an old saying that those who dig a pit for others fall into it themselves. How does the saying apply to the lesson?

Make the relation of love of God and love of country natural. Do not strain to bring in subjects that do not seem to lend themselves to the week's work. Make the best of this opportunity to point out what a splendid citizen a Catholic ought to be, considering that he loves all things in and for God. He can pray for his country, he can work for his country, he can die for his country.

The story of Joan of Arc shows clearly this combination. Many of the saints worked for the welfare of their country in heroic ways. Refer to the Biblical story in the course of the week, in order not to lose the connection.

Can You Answer These Questions?

1. Mardochai was a Jew and knew that he should bend his knee (that is, pay divine honor) to no one but God.

2. The First Commandment tells that we must adore God alone.

3. We adore God by faith, hope, and charity, and by prayer and sacrifice (that is, by honoring Him as our Maker, by bowing to His will, by admitting that we are His creatures and that He can do with us what He wills).

The First Commandment forbids us to give to creatures the honor that is due to God alone. (Explain if it is necessary here.)

Teacher's References:
  The Holy Bible, Esther, iii, vii.
  Teacher's Handbook to Bible History, "Esther," pp. 186–188.
  Catholic Action Series, Book III, "Catholic Action and Citizenship," Chap. VII.
Teacher's Notes:

Lesson 59

Fourth Week in May

Aim: The story of Judith aims to show the trust which her people put in her and how she saved the people of Israel from defeat and death. It also teaches us at the same time the value of people who can be relied upon to act according to right principles.

Preparation: Teach the words: Nĭn′ĭvĕ, Hŏlofer′nĕs, Bĕthuli′a.

As we saw in the last lesson, God sometimes makes use of a good woman to do great things for Him. In our new lesson we shall hear of another woman whom God inspired to save her people, the Jews. Why was God always helping the Jews in spite of their many sins? They were His Chosen People. He had promised them that the Redeemer would come from their nation. From whose family or house was He to come? Find one of Isaias' prophecies to prove your answer.

Read Lesson 59

Discuss some of the more difficult passages in order to make sure that the children understand them.

Explain what it meant to cut off the water supply of a city. What would happen in our large cities if they were walled in and no one could get in or out?

Why did Judith say that the people tempted the Lord?

The beautiful words, "You are the glory of Jerusalem, you are the joy of Israel, you are the honor of our people," are now applied to the Blessed Virgin by the Church. Call attention to Judith's piety and firm trust in God. Notice her words, "Give glory to God, because He is good, because His mercy lasts forever." She does not take the credit herself. She knows that God gave her the strength and courage to save her people! Have the pupils memorize them.

Ask Yourself the Following Questions:

Discuss the questions thoroughly and stress especially the point that God sees us and knows what we do.

The problems bring out reliability as a desirable character trait, rather than the undesirability of the opposite fault. In the problems make a great deal of the children who have proved themselves reliable, without making any direct application to the class. Let the lesson sink in by itself. Point out also that people who are true to God and to their Church can be depended upon to be true to others also and to be reliable in their work. We can see this in the story of Judith. They know that God sees them and that He will reward or punish them.

Teacher's References:

The Holy Bible, Judith vii–xiv.

Teacher's Handbook to Bible History, "Judith," pp. 171–172.

Catholic Action Series, Book II, "The Sermon on the Mount," pp. 413–426.

Teacher's Notes:

Test for Unit VII

Can you find who said these words?

1. "You are the glory of Jerusalem, you are the joy of Israel, you are the honor of our people." (Israelites)

2. "And thou, Bethlehem Ephrata, art a little one among the thousands of Juda: out of thee shall He come forth unto Me that is to be the ruler in Israel." (Micheas v. 2)

3. "If you have much, give a great deal; if you have little, give willingly even a little." (Tobias)

4. "Naked I came to earth, and naked I shall return." (Job)

5. "See that you never do to others what you do not wish others to do to you." (Tobias)

6. "Behold, a virgin shall conceive and bear a son and His name shall be called Emmanuel." (Isaias)

7. "Wherever you shall go, I will go; and where you shall live, I also will live." (Ruth)

8. "A fool laughs at the instruction of his father." (Solomon)

9. "Love the Lord your God with your whole heart, with your whole soul, and with your whole strength." (Moses)

10. "O all you that pass by the way, attend and see, if there be any sorrow like to my sorrow." (Jeremias)

11. "Give me, O Lord, an understanding heart, so that I may be able to judge Your people and to tell good from evil." (Solomon)

12. "Go to Joseph and do all that he shall say." (Pharao)

13. "Lift up your eyes and look to the north and to the south, to the east and to the west. All the land which you see, I will give to you and to your children forever." (God)

14. "Behold, I Myself will seek My sheep and will visit them." (God)

15. "Speak, Lord, for your servant hears." (Samuel)

UNIT VIII

WAITING FOR THE KING
Time: Two weeks in June.

Feasts to Remember

June   5,   St. Boniface, Apostle of Germany
  11,   St. Barnabas, Apostle
  13,   St. Anthony of Padua
  21,   St. Aloysius Gonzaga
  24,   Nativity of St. John the Baptist
  (When St. John saw Jesus walking along the road, he said: "Behold the Lamb of God, behold Him, who taketh away the sins of the world." What prophet first called the Redeemer "Lamb of God"?)
  29,   SS. Peter and Paul, Apostles
    Corpus Christi
    Feast of the Sacred Heart
  (Remind the pupils of the more important feasts to be remembered during the summer, especially the Feast of the Assumption, which is a holyday of obligation.)
The Unit Introduction:
  Read the introduction with the class. Recall to the minds of the pupils the words of Jacob, foretelling that the scepter should not pass out of Juda's hands until He should come who was the Promised of all nations. Have them find the story (Lesson 29). Turn back also to Lesson 55 and the Introduction to Unit VI for a review of the Babylonian captivity. Ask such questions as the following:
  Who was the King that the Jews were waiting for?
  How did they know He was to be a king (Lesson 54)?
  What made them so sure that He was coming soon?

Lessons 60, 61, and 62

First Week in June

Aim: Four thousand years have passed, four thousand years of waiting and longing and praying. The time of Redemption is drawing near. Aim to make the children realize the importance of the moment.

Preparation: Plan to make the closing lessons as effective as you possibly can. Create the right atmosphere. Very appropriate here would be an Advent hymn that expresses in both words and melody, longing for the Redeemer. Connect the thought, then, with our own preparation for the Birthday of the King during the season of Advent.

Read Lesson 60 and answer the questions.

Can You Answer These Questions?

1. They who are expected to die should receive the sacrament of Extreme Unction.

Speak of this sacrament and develop it according to the needs of the children. Teach them to prepare a table for Extreme Unction. A set of rubber stamps can be obtained for the purpose from the Catechetical Guild, St. Paul ($1). Cut-outs of the various articles may also be made by the children and mounted on heavy cardboard.

2. After death the soul goes to heaven, hell, or purgatory.

3. Purgatory is a place where those suffer for a time who die with only venial sins on their souls.

4. We can shorten our own purgatory in a number of ways:

a) By keeping away from sin as much as possible.

b) By praying, doing good works, hearing Mass, going to the sacraments, and gaining indulgences. (Explain very simply how the children can gain an indulgence.) Teach a few simple ejaculations for the children to say, such as, "My Jesus, mercy"; "Jesus, Mary, and Joseph, I give you my heart and my soul." Call attention also to the fact that there is an indulgence for learning the Catechism (see *Catholic School Journal,* October, 1933, p. 233).

Read Lesson 61

This lesson summarizes once more, the history of the Jews. It should be read carefully a number of times, so that the children can repeat it in their own words.

Lesson 62

Aim: This lesson aims at giving a historical setting for the central event of all human history — the coming of the Redeemer.

Preparation: If possible have a map of the Roman Empire on hand, so as to show the children the size of Chanaan as compared with the whole of the Roman Empire. A blackboard sketch of the map will do.

There are many activities suggested in "Interesting Things to Do." Read them over and plan which of them you wish to carry out. They should aid in giving the children a better understanding of the lesson itself and of conditions as they existed at the time when Christ came.

Read Lesson 62

Discuss the lesson paragraph by paragraph. Paragraph 1 shows what a small proportion of people believed in the one true God.

Paragraph 2 shows the working of divine Providence. We saw it clearly in the lesson about Joseph and his brothers.

Paragraph 3 calls for a backward glance to find the reason why the Romans were called in to help the Jews. (Lesson 60.)

Paragraph 4 shows how God made use of the Romans to prepare the way for Christianity. Discuss how good roads helped the spread of Christianity.

Paragraph 5 may well be supplemented by a reading of the Gospel for the Christmas Midnight Mass.

Paragraph 6 should be discussed more at length, showing how the Apostles carried on the work of Christ. Christ founded the Church and promised that the gates of hell should not prevail against it.

Enter into the spirit of joy which the final quotation should awaken in all of us at the thoughts of the things that await those who are faithful to the Redeemer.

Interesting Things for You to Do:

1. Recall again that these activities must have an intimate bearing on the lesson itself.

2. Let the children also repeat the connection these places have with the coming of the Redeemer.

3. *Lesson 46.* David lived in Bethlehem. Mary and Joseph were the descendants of David. Therefore they had to go to Bethlehem to be enrolled.

4. *Lesson 43.* Ruth was the great grandmother of David.

5. Have someone relate the story of the Wise Men. Pictures of the different incidents would be very appropriate.

6. Repeat, also, the Apostles' Creed.

7 and 8. You will, no doubt, have to give the children some help in these problems.

Good roads made travel easy. One language understood by all made it easy to spread the teachings of the Redeemer faster. All nations being under one ruler, it was easier to go from one country to the other without being disturbed. Peace in the world also aided the rapid spread of Christianity without disturbance. The Jews scattered in different countries prepared the way for belief in the one, true God.

9. Saviour, Jesus, Emmanuel, Prince of Peace, Son of God.

10. Try to give the children something of that feeling of joy that should animate them at the thought of heaven.

11. These little talks, may, of course, be omitted or made very short.

12. Teach or review the seasons of the ecclesiastical year.

13. It would be well, in preparation for the vacation days, to speak somewhat at length on the use of the Catholic calendar in the home, especially for finding important days of the ecclesiastical year. Note especially the 15th of August, a holyday of obligation, and the fish indicating whenever there is a day of abstinence.

15. If there is time, review in short the Prophets, their work, and their wonderful sayings.

16. Make this an interesting dialog to bring out the setting and conditions of the times.

17. A period for written language work may be used for these or similar letters.

18. The *Gregory Hymnal* offers good material.

Teacher's References:

The Holy Bible, II Mach. xii.

Teacher's Handbook to Bible History, "Judas Machabeus," pp. 192–194; "The Fullness of Time," pp. 194–197.

Catholic Action Series, Book II, "Advent," "Preparation for Coming of Christ," pp. 197–198.

Teacher's Notes:

Test for Unit VIII

Find the name below and put it next to the sentence that describes the person.

Built the Ark. (Noe)

Gave all the animals in paradise their names. (Adam)

Tempted Eve to eat of the forbidden fruit. (The serpent — devil)

The King of Salem, priest of the Most High God. (Melchisedech)

Entertained three Guests. (Abraham)

Turned into a statue of salt. (Wife of Lot)

Was to be offered as a sacrifice by his father. (Isaac)

Went to find a wife for Isaac. (Eliezer)

Took the birthright from his brother. (Jacob)

Met Jacob at the well and later became his wife. (Rachel)

Was sold as a slave. (Joseph)

The youngest son of Jacob. (Benjamin)

Did not complain when he lost all his children and goods. (Job)

Heard the voice of God from a burning bush. (Moses)

Made a golden calf for the people of Israel. (Aaron)

Drowned in the Red Sea while following the Israelites. (Pharao)

Led the people back into the Promised Land. (Josue)

Called to be a leader while he was threshing wheat. (Gedeon)

Went out into the field to glean after the reapers. (Ruth)

Was brought to the high priest Heli to serve in the temple. (Samuel)

The first king of Israel. (Saul)

The boy who killed a giant. (David)

The king who built a beautiful temple to the Lord. (Solomon)

The prophet who brought back rain after three years. (Elias)

The man who was cured of leprosy by Eliseus. (Naaman)

The man who was cured of his blindness by his son. (Tobias)

The angel who went with the young Tobias. (Raphael)

The greatest of all prophets. (Isaias)

The prophet who wept over the ruins of Jerusalem. (Jeremias)

The prophet who said that the Redeemer would be born in Bethlehem. (Micheas)

The prophet who saw dead bones rise up and form a great army. (Ezechiel)

The man whom the lions would not devour. (Daniel)

The beautiful queen who saved the Jews from death. (Esther)

The woman who cut off the head of Holofernes. (Judith)

The "Hammerer." (Judas Machabeus)

The pagan nation that was called to help the Jews settle their quarrels. (Romans)

The emperor who wanted all his people counted. (Augustus)

The woman who believed the serpent more than God. (Eve)

The mother of the Redeemer. (Mary)

The Spouse of the Blessed Virgin Mary. (St. Joseph)

1. Jacob		21. Eve	
2. Pharao		22. Isaias	
3. David		23. Romans	
4. Noe		24. Joseph	
5. Isaac		25. Judas Machabeus	
6. Solomon		26. Ruth	
7. Micheas		27. Esther	
8. Benjamin		28. Naaman	
9. Elias		29. Daniel	
10. Adam		30. Samuel	
11. Mary		31. St. Joseph	
12. Abraham		32. Job	
13. Judith		33. Serpent–Devil	
14. Josue		34. Moses	
15. Augustus		35. Jeremias	
16. Eliezer		36. Melchisedech	
17. Wife of Lot		37. Raphael	
18. David		38. Aaron	
19. Ezechiel		39. Tobias	
20. Gedeon		40. Rebecca	

TEACHER'S REFERENCES

While the teacher is urged to read widely in preparation for her daily work, there are only four books mentioned specifically throughout, in order to simplify the problem of purchasing additional texts. The references most frequently used are:

The Holy Bible: This is the authentic and inspired source for the historical events related in the text and should be read above all others.

Urban, *Teacher's Handbook to Bible History.* Joseph F. Wagner, Inc., New York. This book has been selected principally for its explanation of and commentary on each lesson.

Bandas, *Biblical Questions.* Bruce Publishing Co., Milwaukee, Wis., 1935. This book contains answers to questions frequently asked by students of Sacred Scripture about Biblical incidents and passages difficult to understand. The information is for the teacher's own enrichment rather than for direct use in the classroom.

Campion, *Catholic Action Series,* a high-school text in three books. These books have been selected for their practical application of religious principles to everyday life. The busy teacher will find the short and simple readings very helpful and stimulating.

Other Helpful References:

The Catholic School Journal. Bruce Publishing Company, Milwaukee, Wis.

The Journal of Religious Instruction. De Paul University, Chicago, Ill.

Art Education Through Religion, Books I to VIII. Gertrude M. McMunigle, Mentzer, Bush & Co., Chicago, Ill. This is a set of graded books in art work for children which correlates religion and art.

The Music Hour, Catholic Edition, in five books for grades 1 to 9. Silver Burdett & Co., Chicago, Ill. These graded books offer a variety of songs, religious hymns, and Gregorian chant very helpful in the teaching of religion as the dominant factor in everyday life.

The St. Gregory Hymnal. The St. Gregory Guild, 1705 Rittenhouse St., Philadelphia, Pa.

Books for Children:

Good News for God's Children. Gales, 64 pages, 30 beautifully colored Bible pictures, 15 cents. Catechetical Guild, St. Paul, Minn.

The Best Gift. Mass Book for children, with simple prayers expressing the thought of the Mass Liturgy. 7 cents per single copies. Catechetical Guild, St. Paul, Minn.

The Our Father for Little Ones, a book of verse with ten beautiful illustrations in color. 10 cents. Catechetical Guild, St. Paul, Minn.

A Child's Garden of Religion Stories. Matimore, Macmillan Company.

Wonder Stories of God's People. Matimore, Macmillan Co.

Six O'Clock Saints. Windham, Sheed and Ward, New York.

Medal Stories, by the Daughters of Charity, Brown, Morrison Co., Inc., Lynchburg, Va., 1933. These stories can also be obtained in the five-and-ten-cent stores in ten-cent editions.

Little Queen, by a Sister of Notre Dame, Ad-Vantage Press, Cincinnati, Ohio.

Story of St. Francis of Assisi, Sister M. Eleanore.

Stations of the Cross for Children. Paulist Press, New York.

Pictures:

The Perry Picture Co., Malden, Mass.

New York Sunday School Commission, 416 Lafayette St., New York. (Tissot Pictures.)

The University Prints, 10 Boyd St., Newton, Mass.

The Art Extension Society, Westport, Conn.

The Catechetical Guild, St. Paul, Minn.

Other Helpful Material for Religious Instruction:

Creative Education Co., Coughlin Bldg., Mankato, Minn.

Large colored Mass Charts with explanation.

Rubber-stamp outfit of articles for the Mass and pictures of saints.

Catechetical Guild, St. Paul, Minn.

The Mass, thirty rubber stamps, $5.

Sick-call outfit, rubber stamps, $1.

Wooden Altar and miniature articles used at Mass.

Pictures and other instructional material.

Co-op Parish Activities, Effingham, Ill.

Pictures, films, projects, charts, and every variety of instructional material. Send for catalog.

RESOURCE LIST

We have collected on the following pages a comprehensive list of all the recommended resources found in this manual. Based on their content and/or their frequent use in this series (often across more than one grade level) we have indicated the most essential of these with an asterisk (*), while resources which may be found on the internet are marked with a cross (†).

Fourth Grade Teacher Resources

*† *The Holy Bible.*

† *The Catholic Encyclopedia,* (New York: Robert Appleton Company, 1907-1912).

**Art Education through Religion,* Mary G. McMunigle (New York: Mentzer, Bush & Company, 1931).

Biblical Questions (Vol. 1: Old Testament), Rev. Rudolph G. Bandas (Milwaukee: The Bruce Publishing Company, 1934).

The Catholic Action Series, Books 1-3, Rev. Raymond J. Campion (New York: William H. Sadlier, Inc., 1928).

Introduction to the Bible, Rev. John Joseph Laux (New York: Benziger Brothers, 1932).

**Practical Aids for Catholic Teachers,* Sr. Mary Aurelia, O.S.F., M.A. and Rev. Felix M. Kirsch, O.M.Cap., Litt.D. (New York: Benziger Brothers, 1928).

† *Teacher's Handbook to Bible History,* Rev. A. Urban (New York: Joseph F. Wagner, 1905).

Fourth Grade Student Readers

(This list is provided for reference purposes; the majority of recommended readings from these books has been included in a newly published anthology reader to accompany this series.)

The American Cardinal Reader, Book Four, Edith M. McLaughlin (New York: Benziger Brothers, 1929).

The American Fourth Reader for Catholic Schools, The School Sisters of Notre Dame (Boston: D.C. Heath and Company, 1924).

Cathedral Basic Readers, Book Four, Rev. John A. O'Brien, Ph.D. (Chicago: Scott, Foresman and Company, 1932).

Catholic National Readers, Book Four (New York: Benziger Brothers, 1890s).

The Catholic Youth Fourth Reader, Rena A. Weider, B.S. and Msgr. Charles F. McEvoy, A.M., LL.D. (Chicago: The John C. Winston Company, 1930).

Child-Story Readers Fourth Reader, Frank N. Freeman, Eleanor M Johnson (Chicago: Lyons and Carnahan, Publishers, 1929).

The Corona Readers, Book 4, James H. Fassett (Boston: Ginn and Company, 1926).

De la Salle Readers Fourth Grade, Brothers of the Christian Schools (New York: St. Joseph's Normal Institute, 1915).

The Ideal Catholic Reader, Fourth Reader, A Sister of St. Joseph (New York: The MacMillan Company, 1916).

The Laidlaw Readers Book Four, Dressel, Veverka and Graff (Chicago: Laidlaw Brothers Publishers, 1921).

The Marywood Readers: The Story Cargo (Fourth Reader), Sister Mary Estelle (New York: The MacMillan Company, 1932).

Misericordia Readers Fourth Reader, The Sisters of Mercy (Chicago: Rand McNally & Company, 1933).

The Rosary Readers Fourth Reader, Sister Mary Henry, O.S.D. (Boston: Ginn and Company, 1929).

Standard Catholic Readers, Fourth Reader, Mary E. Doyle (New York: American Book Company, 1909).

Additional Student Reading for Fourth Grade

Bible Stories for Children, Sister Anna Louise, S.S.J. (New York: Schwartz, Kirwin & Fauss, 1919-1935).

The Bible Story, Johnson, Hannan and Sister M. Dominica (New York: Benziger Brothers, 1931).

*A Child's Garden of Religion Stories, Rev. P. Henry Matimore, S.T.D. (New York: The Macmillan Company, 1929).

*Wonder Stories of God's People, Rev. P. Henry Matimore, S.T.D. (New York: The Macmillan Company, 1929).

THE HIGHWAY TO HEAVEN SERIES

Prepared in the Catechetical Institute of Marquette University
(In co-operation with a group of Priests and Sisters teaching in the elementary schools)

GRADE	TEXT	MANUAL CURRICULUM IN RELIGION *(1st to 8th Grade inclusive)*
1	**THE BOOK OF THE HOLY CHILD** By *Sister Mary Bartholomew, O.S.F.* 96 pages	First Grade Teachers Plan Book and Manual
2	**THE LIFE OF MY SAVIOR** By a School Sister of Notre Dame 196 pages	Second Grade Teachers Plan Book and Manual
3	**THE LIFE OF THE SOUL** Prepared in the Catechetical Institute of Marquette University *Edward A. Fitzpatrick, Ph.D.* Educational Director 144 pages	Third Grade Teachers Plan Book and Manual
4	**BEFORE CHRIST CAME** By a School Sister of Notre Dame 256 pages	Fourth Grade Teachers Plan Book and Manual
5	**THE VINE AND THE BRANCHES** By the *Rev. R. G. Bandas,* *Ph.D.Agg., S.T.D. et M.* and a School Sister of Notre Dame 320 pages	Fifth Grade Teachers Plan Book and Manual
6	**THE SMALL MISSAL**	Workbook for the Missal
7 & 8	**THE HIGHWAY TO GOD** Prepared in the Catechetical Institute of Marquette University *Edward A. Fitzpatrick, Ph.D.* Educational Director 420 pages	Practical Problems in Religion By the *Rev. R. G. Bandas,* *Ph.D.Agg., S.T.D. et M.* (Answers problems in text)

www.ingramcontent.com/pod-product-compliance
Lightning Source LLC
LaVergne TN
LVHW051512080426
835509LV00017B/2046